MASTERING CONFIDENCE

Lessons From The Dog Life Coach

Alison Hatton

Introduction

Confidence is like your secret superpower. It's those roots that keep you grounded and help you stand tall, boosting your self-esteem and self-image. With confidence in your corner, you're ready to take on challenges, bounce back from life's difficulties and enjoy stronger relationships. In the professional field it can lead to career advancement. Confidence isn't just about mental strength; it's a stress-buster and a decision-making expert, making life smoother. It even has a hand in your physical well-being.

Do any of these problems resonate with you:

'I often doubt my abilities and hesitate to take on new challenges.'

'I feel like I'm constantly comparing myself to others, and it's eating away at my self-esteem.'

'Criticism and negative feedback knock me down, making it hard to stay confident.'

'I'm paralyzed by fear when it comes to taking risks and pursuing my dreams.'

'I'm tired of feeling like an imposter in my own life and career.'

The key to great confidence is understanding your strengths and weaknesses while keeping that unwavering belief in your potential to grow and succeed. Now, you might be wondering, *How can we develop more of this amazing confidence?* I've spent decades exploring the world of personal development, searching for the most profound and transformative life lessons. And guess what? Some of the most powerful wisdom comes from the hearts of our dogs. In the world of self-help and personal growth one of the most valuable sources of wisdom is right beside you, wagging its tail and looking at you with eyes full of love. Dogs are the silent teachers, leading by example and imparting wisdom that, when we take it to heart, can transform our lives in the most incredible ways. In this book we'll explore the incredible attributes of dogs, including presence, loyalty, fearlessness and courage amongst many others. Applying these traits to our own lives acts as stepping-stones on our path towards unshakable confidence.

Dogs are true mindfulness masters, living fully in the present, finding joy in simple moments, and reminding us that life's beauty lies in the every day. They exude unshakable self-love and confidence, inspiring us to embrace ourselves as we are. They fearlessly dive into the unknown, showing us the essence of courage. This lesson in boldness is a nudge to face our own fears and doubts with unwavering bravery and do it anyway. So, how can we apply these remarkable lessons to our own lives and, in doing so, build that unshakable confidence we all desire?

As we embark on this journey together, we'll uncover the answers to this question and many more and discover the power of embracing our inner courage. This book isn't just about learning from dogs; it's about embracing their teachings and applying them to your life in a practical way. At the end of each chapter you'll find a set of exercises designed to help you apply these valuable lessons. So, by the time you reach the last page of this book, you won't just understand why dogs make exceptional life coaches; you'll also possess a versatile toolkit loaded with practical exercises and insights, enabling you to establish resolute self-confidence and make the leap from surviving to thriving.

CHAPTER 1: TRUST

In the heart of every dog there exists a profound quality, that of trust. In their eyes there is an unwavering belief in the goodness of the world. They place their trust not only in us, their human, but also in the simple beauty of each new day. Dogs remind us that trust is a heartfelt connection. Their trust isn't conditional; it's a gift that enriches our lives. Whether they are eagerly awaiting our return or simply resting their heads in our laps, dogs demonstrate the art of trust in its purest form.

Dogs, with their unwavering trust, can teach us valuable lessons about self-confidence. Trust is a vital element in not only building self-assurance but also maintaining it. Have you ever thought about the art of self-trust? It's about believing in your own capacity, resilience and wisdom to face life's ups and downs. Just like dogs trust the world around them – from the people they meet to the places they explore – we, too, can develop trust in ourselves. Self-trust doesn't rely on external validation. It's an inner sense, a deep belief that comes from within. Have you considered how much we can learn from dogs' unwavering trust in their instincts and abilities? They wholeheartedly believe in themselves, embrace every adventure and tackle challenges without hesitation. Can you imagine having that kind of unshakable belief in your own abilities, even in the face of uncertainty?

How you ever thought about how self-trust shapes our self-esteem and overall confidence? It's not just blind faith but an inner journey, developing your intuition to navigate life. Unlike us, dogs don't dive into self-doubt or overthinking; they step forward with unwavering self-reliance, trusting their gut instinct. How can we adopt this mindset? Picture a dog tackling life – be it leaping for a ball or exploring new places – with self-belief, unruffled by 'what ifs' or anxiety. They trust their instincts, guiding them with unwavering confidence. With practice, we can use the same self-trust to overcome difficulties and stay true to ourselves.

Confidence finds its roots in self-trust, a belief in your own capabilities, resilience and wisdom to navigate life's problems and stay true to your values and purpose. When you embrace self-trust, you move through life with a natural understanding that you're well-prepared to confront any situation. It's about having solid faith in your capacity not just to withstand challenges but to emerge from them as a stronger, wiser individual. You become less vulnerable to self-doubt or the urge to second-guess your choices. Instead, you face life's trials with a quiet confidence, fully aware that your inner compass, your intuition, is finely tuned, and your decisions match with your values and ambitions.

Unshakable confidence lies in the trust you invest in your own capabilities. It's a belief that you possess the skills, talents and the knowledge needed to shine in various aspects of life. Confidence springs from the authentic belief that you have what it takes to succeed. It's not a blind or unfounded confidence; it's set in your awareness of your skills and talents. This self-assurance doesn't stop you from experiencing difficulties or having to face obstacles; instead, it allows you to overcome them. You're more inclined to choose opportunities for growth, take calculated risks and explore new ideas. This positive mindset not only opens doors to new possibilities but also increases your ability to learn and adapt.

Unshakable confidence thrives on resilience. It's the belief in your ability to bounce back from life's challenges and setbacks, emerging even stronger. It's about trusting that, despite problems, your worth remains intact and your goals remain intact. This trust transforms challenges into stepping-stones, failures into valuable lessons and setbacks into opportunities for growth. It's like a dog chasing a ball, coming up against obstacles, pausing briefly but never giving up. How can you adopt this firm determination in the face of life's hurdles? Resilience acts as your internal compass, guiding you through life's uncertainties, established in the belief that you can regain your footing after temporary setbacks. Developing this belief in your ability to persevere becomes a source of inner strength, helping you to navigate life's difficulties and emerge with a newfound wisdom, changing your outlook and approach to challenges.

Cultivating confidence rests on the trust in your decision-making ability. It's not about blind faith or random choices; it's about believing in your capacity to evaluate situations, weighing alternatives and making choices that align with your values and dreams. How can you boost your trust in your judgement as a reliable compass guiding you towards your goals? Think of a dog in the woods, choosing the path to its desired destination with unwavering confidence. Trusting your decision-making is like having that guide for life's complex choices. With faith in your ability to decide, you act decisively, even in uncertainty. This trust becomes your driving force, allowing you to pursue your goals with a staunch determination, knowing your choices are rooted in wisdom and self-assurance.

It is important to have unwavering trust in your self-worth, recognising your inherent value remains steadfast, unchanged by external judgements. It forms the core of strong self-esteem. This kind of confidence comes from deep-rooted self-assuredness, grounded in the understanding that you hold intrinsic worth, deserving love, respect and happiness simply by being. To strengthen your self-confidence and self-esteem, picture a carefree dog, unfazed by social judgements, embracing its unique qualities and intrinsic worth. This trust in self-worth echoes innate self-assuredness, allowing you to be less reliant on external opinions. It invites you to embrace your strengths and imperfections, your victories and setbacks, with self-compassion, recognising that you're always evolving and learning, and your worth isn't tied to achieving perfection.

Dogs possess an inherent trust in the world and in themselves. Their trust is not conditional or dependent on external validation – it's a pure gift that strengthens our connection with them and serves as a foundation for their unwavering loyalty. Just as dogs trust in their instincts and abilities; you, too, can learn to trust yourself, your abilities and your unique worth. This will provide the inner strength and resilience needed to weather life's ups and downs while maintaining a positive and determined outlook. Building and nurturing trust is a key aspect of personal growth and the development of unwavering self-assurance. Take a look at the exercises that follow. Incorporating these exercises into your routine can significantly contribute to building unshakable confidence. Over time, you'll notice positive changes in how you see yourself and your ability to face life's challenges with resilience and self-assuredness. Remember that your journey towards confidence starts with trust – in yourself.

Exercise 1: Resilience Building

The aim of this exercise is to nurture resilience and trust in your ability to overcome obstacles. It will help you develop resilience by encouraging you to view setbacks as opportunities for growth. Trust in your ability to overcome obstacles is strengthened as you work through challenges and learn from them. Over time, this practice will enhance your overall confidence.

Instructions

When faced with a setback or challenge, take out your journal. Reflect on the situation and your initial feelings about it. Write down your thoughts without judgement.

Now, consider how you can bounce back from this setback. What lessons can you learn from it? How can you emerge stronger and wiser?

Write down a plan of action or specific steps you can take to address the challenge.

Revisit your journal entry periodically to track your progress, and adapt your approach if needed.

Exercise 2: Decision-Making Confidence

The aim of this exercise is to build trust in your decision-making abilities. By examining your decisions and their outcomes, you'll enhance your confidence in your ability to make sound judgements and effective choices.

Instructions

Think about a recent decision you made, whether big or small. Write down the decision, your reasons for making it and the expected outcomes.

Reflect on the actual results of your decision. Were they in line with your expectations?

If the outcomes were positive, acknowledge your good judgement. If they were less favourable, focus on what you've learned from the experience.

Repeat this process with different decisions to practice and reinforce your trust in your decision-making skills.

Exercise 3: Self-Worth Reflection

This exercise reinforces your trust in your self-worth and empowers you to embrace your strengths and imperfections with self-compassion. It strengthens your understanding that you are valuable, regardless of external opinions or circumstances.

Instructions

Find a quiet space where you can reflect without distractions.

Close your eyes and take a few deep breaths to centre yourself.

Focus on your inner self and your core value as a human being.

Repeat positive affirmations such as 'I am valuable,' 'I deserve love and respect,' and 'My worth is unshaken by external judgements.'

Whenever self-doubt or negative self-perceptions surface, consciously replace them with these affirmations.

Practice this self-worth reflection regularly, ideally daily.
Incorporating these exercises into your routine can significantly contribute to building unshakable confidence. Over time, you'll

notice positive changes in how you see yourself and your ability to face life's challenges with resilience and self-assuredness. Remember that your journey towards confidence starts with trust – in yourself.

CHAPTER 2: FEARLESSNESS AND COURAGE

Dogs show us that courage isn't about the absence of fear; it's about having the strength to confront those fears head-on. Picture that puppy, just starting to venture out into the great unknown. Every new sight, sound and scent is an adventure waiting to be enjoyed. But then there's us; we often have inner fears and hidden inner beliefs that lurk in the shadows, holding us back from fully embracing life. So, how do we go about transforming these inner fears into the very stepping-stones that will lead us towards courage and confidence?

Dogs are like life adventurers, always ready to jump into the unknown and flourish outside their comfort zones. When you take your dog to a new park, their excitement is infectious as they explore every scent, tree and patch of grass like it's treasure, waiting to be discovered. They teach us that there's magic in venturing beyond what we know. Just as they do, we, too, can find a world full of amazing possibilities when we step beyond our comfort zones. Courage is the key, moving us from a fixed mindset to one of growth and self-improvement. Just like dogs that face challenges without fear, we can learn to gather our inner determination, using their resilience as an example. How can you apply your dog's fearless approach to life's challenges? What's one step you can take today to travel beyond your comfort zone and embrace personal growth with courage and determination?

'Feel the fear and do it anyway' is a powerful saying that sums up the essence of courage and personal growth. It's about acknowledging and embracing fear as a natural human emotion while still taking action and moving forward. Have you ever thought about the first part of this saying, 'Feel the fear'? It emphasises the importance of recognising and accepting fear. After all, fear is a fundamental human emotion, and everyone experiences it at various points in life. Instead of denying or suppressing fear, we should acknowledge it as a valid response to uncertainty, change or challenges. But what about understanding where your fear comes from? Sometimes, fear is a signal that we are stepping out of our comfort zone, which can lead to personal growth. Other times, it might be an irrational fear based on past experiences or negative beliefs. By understanding the nature of our fear, we can address it more effectively. So, have you considered what fears might be holding you back from personal growth?

The second part of this saying, 'do it anyway,' emphasises the importance of taking action despite feeling fear. Courage is not the absence of fear; it's the willingness to move forward despite its presence. Have you ever considered that courage isn't about being fearless but about taking that step into the unknown? Whether it's pursuing a new career, starting a challenging project or facing a difficult conversation, courage is required. Have you thought about where you might need to summon courage in your life? How has taking action despite fear led to personal growth in the past? When you feel the fear, remind yourself of the growth that can come from taking action anyway. With one small step a day, you can confront fear and build your courage.

Courage isn't the absence of fear; it's the willingness to act despite it. Have you ever considered how this kind of courage can bolster your resilience? Think about it; when we confront our fears, whether they relate to public speaking, taking on new responsibilities or venturing outside our comfort zone, we gradually take apart mental barriers. Each time we conquer a fear, it's proof that we're capable of handling challenges. Can you recall a specific fear you conquered that made you feel more capable and confident? Dogs thrive beyond their comfort zones, and they encourage us to do the same. When we explore new things we unearth hidden strengths and talents we didn't know we possessed. This process of self-discovery significantly contributes to our self-assurance. Overcoming fear and demonstrating courage sets in motion a positive feedback loop. As we achieve small victories, our confidence grows and we become better equipped to tackle bigger challenges. Can you recall moments when you bounced back from setbacks and failures, realising they don't define you? Facing your fears is a crucial step in the journey towards confidence. The connection between handling adversity and your self-esteem and confidence is clear. Navigating fear-inducing situations reinforces your belief in your abilities, providing evidence that you can handle adversity and, in turn, boosts your self-esteem and confidence.

In the world of dogs, they teach us that courage is not the absence of fear but the strength to confront it. Stepping out of our comfort zones, much like dogs do, leads us to a world of endless possibilities. The saying 'Feel the fear and do it anyway' captures the essence of courage, urging us to acknowledge our fears and take action. This journey of confronting fears and demonstrating courage breaks down mental barriers, boosts self-esteem and uncovers hidden strengths. By following in the fearless footsteps of dogs, we start walking a path towards building confidence, and by engaging in the following exercises you'll gradually transform your inner fears into stepping-stones towards courage and unwavering confidence.

Exercise 1: Fear Assessment

The aim of this exercise is to gain a deeper understanding of your fears, identify their sources and find out if they are delaying your personal growth and confidence. By assessing your fears and their impact on your life, you can gain understanding, develop strategies to confront them, and build the courage and confidence needed to thrive outside your comfort zone.

Instructions

Set aside time and find a quiet and comfortable space where you can focus without distractions. Allocate twenty to thirty minutes for this exercise. You'll need a notebook or journal and a pen to write down your thoughts and reflections.

Begin by reflecting on the fears that currently affect you. These could be related to your career, relationships, personal development or any other aspect of your life. Write down each fear as a separate entry in your journal.

For each fear you've listed, dig deeper. Ask yourself questions like:

'Where does this fear come from?'

'Is it based on a past negative experience?'

'Is this fear rational or irrational?'

'How does this fear make me feel?'

Try to pinpoint the source or trigger of each fear. Is it rooted in a past traumatic event, a childhood experience or is it something you can't clearly identify? Write down your findings.

Consider whether each fear is limiting your personal growth or hindering your confidence. Write down your observations on how these fears affect your actions, decisions and mindset.

If you've identified irrational fears, challenge them with rational thinking. Ask yourself if the fear is based on facts or assumptions. Write down counterarguments to irrational fears.

Create an action plan. Decide what steps you can take to confront and overcome these fears. Be specific and realistic in your planning.

Establish achievable goals related to facing and conquering your fears. These goals should align with your action plan and contribute to your personal growth.

Regularly revisit your fear assessment and action plan. Monitor your progress in overcoming fears and achieving your goals. Use this exercise as a tool for self-awareness and personal development.

Exercise 2: Step Outside Your Comfort Zone

This exercise encourages you to confront your fears and expand your comfort zone by taking a small but meaningful step towards something you've been avoiding due to fear. This will help you build courage and confidence in the face of challenges. Remember that courage is not the absence of fear but the willingness to act despite it.

Instructions

Begin by reflecting on areas of your life where you've been avoiding taking action due to fear. This could be related to personal growth, career, relationships, or any aspect that feels challenging.

Choose one specific fear-based avoidance that you want to address in this exercise. It should be something that, if confronted, would contribute to your personal growth and confidence. Write it down.

Break down the chosen avoidance into smaller, manageable steps. For example, if your fear is public speaking, the first step might be researching public speaking classes in your area.

Take the first small step you've identified and start researching or planning for it. If it's signing up for a public speaking class, find classes near you, check their schedules and write down contact information.

Establish a realistic deadline for completing this step. Setting a time frame adds accountability and prevents procrastination.

Take action according to your plan. In the case of public speaking, contact the class organisers and enrol. If it's a different fear-based avoidance, carry out the corresponding step you've outlined.

Accept that stepping outside your comfort zone may be uncomfortable, and that's okay. Embrace the discomfort as a sign of growth and courage.

After completing the step, take some time to reflect on your experience. How did you feel before, during and after taking action? What did you learn from this small step outside your comfort zone?

If the first step felt manageable, consider repeating this exercise by tackling the next step in your plan. Gradually, you can work your way up to more significant challenges.

Regardless of the outcome, celebrate your courage and willingness to confront your fears. Recognise that each step outside your comfort zone is a victory on your journey to building confidence.

Continue to identify and address fear-based avoidances in your life. With each small step, you'll expand your comfort zone, develop courage and gain confidence to face even bigger challenges.

◆ ◆ ◆

Exercise 3: Embrace Failure

By embracing failure as a stepping-stone to success and recognising the growth opportunities it presents, you'll become more resilient and self-assured. This exercise encourages a mindset shift that can contribute significantly to your overall confidence. Remember that failure is not the end but a crucial part of the journey towards achieving your goals.

Instructions

Take some time to reflect on your past failures. These can be related to your personal life, career, education or any area where you've faced setbacks.

For each failure you've reflected on, identify the lessons or insights you gained from the experience. How did the failure contribute to your personal growth or lead to new opportunities?

Write down your findings from step 2. Create a list or journal where you record specific examples of how failure has been a catalyst for positive change in your life.

Consider how your perspective on failure has evolved through this exercise. Instead of seeing failure as a negative outcome, view it as a necessary part of the learning process.

Adopt the idea that failure is not a reflection of your worth or competence but a natural part of the journey to success. Embrace the idea that failure can lead to personal and professional growth.

Challenge yourself to take on a new task that you've been avoiding due to the fear of failure. This should be something that pushes your boundaries and offers the potential for growth.

Before starting the challenge, acknowledge that failure is a possibility. Understand that coming up against obstacles and setbacks is normal when trying new things.

With your newfound outlook on failure, take action towards your chosen challenge. Whether it's starting a new project, pursuing a new skill or taking a calculated risk, initiate the process.

As you work on your challenge reflect on your experiences, including any setbacks or failures you encounter. Write down what you learn from these moments.

When faced with setbacks or failures, recognise them as

opportunities for growth and learning. Identify the lessons and insights that come from these experiences.

Celebrate not only your successes but also your ability to embrace failure as a valuable part of your journey. Acknowledge your courage and resilience in the face of challenges.

Continue to apply your transformed perspective on failure to various aspects of your life. Whenever you encounter setbacks, remind yourself of the lessons learned and the potential for growth.

CHAPTER 3: RESILIENCE

Resilience and confidence are close companions on our journey to self-assurance and personal growth, and dogs have loads of wisdom to share on bouncing back from life's setbacks. Whether dealing with health issues, adapting to a new environment or coping with loss, dogs show resilience by their ability to recover, heal and rediscover joy. So, how can these empower us to face life's hurdles? It's about recognising that resilience and confidence are a dynamic duo, working together to fuel our self-assuredness and personal growth. When we confront life's challenges and setbacks with resilience, we lay the foundation for inner strength and self-belief. This newfound strength, in turn, increases our confidence, equipping us to tackle future challenges.

What's the link between resilience and unwavering confidence, and how can the lessons we learn from dogs help us navigate life's ups and downs with greater assurance? Think about resilience for a moment. It's not just reserved for significant challenges; it's a part of everyday life for dogs. Take, for example, a dog patiently waiting for their owner's return, only to be left alone longer than expected. While many of us might feel anxiety or loneliness in such a situation, dogs adapt and hold on to hope. When their owner eventually returns, their tails wag with just as much joy. It's a testament to their resilience in the face of temporary adversity.

Following on from a previous chapter, let's talk about trust again. Dogs trust in their humans, but they also extend that trust to themselves and the world around them. This trust serves as a strong foundation for their resilience. Dogs have an unwavering belief in their own ability to conquer challenges, to navigate the unknown and to discover joy in each and every moment. They place their trust in their instincts, their skills and their resilience to carry them through whatever comes their way. So, what can we learn from this profound trust that dogs have? It's more than just a leap of faith; it's a deeply ingrained conviction that we possess the inner strength to confront the uncertainties of life.

One of the standout qualities that makes dogs amazing is their adaptability in the face of change and unpredictability. Life is full of twists and turns, but dogs have a unique way of teaching us that not only is it possible to embrace the unknown, but it's also a source of growth. Whether they encounter a sudden shift in their daily routine, find themselves in new surroundings or meet unfamiliar faces, dogs approach these changes with a blend of curiosity and an open heart. How do they manage it, and what insights can we gain from their adaptability in handling life's changes? It's not just about following their example; it's about using adaptability as a tool to view change as an opportunity for growth rather than a source of fear. The important thing to remember is that adaptability is a crucial piece of the resilience puzzle. When we can tackle unexpected challenges and setbacks with the same kind of flexibility and open-mindedness that dogs exhibit, we're well on our way to bouncing back and emerging stronger.

Let's explore a fundamental aspect of personal growth – emotional resilience. It plays a significant role in shaping our self-confidence. So, what exactly is emotional resilience? Think of it as your superpower for bouncing back from adversity, maintaining emotional equilibrium during tough times and adapting positively when life throws you a curveball. It's similar to having an inner strength that allows you to pass through life's storms without getting overwhelmed by them. Emotional resilience and self-confidence aren't solo acts; they're a dynamic duo. They work together to improve your overall well-being. Have you ever felt overwhelmed by your own feelings? It's a common experience. Recognising and understanding these emotional responses is the first step in regaining control over how we react to life's challenges. Self-awareness isn't something you're born with or without; it's a skill you can develop and refine over time. Think of it as a muscle you can strengthen. With emotional resilience in your corner, it's like having a safety net to face life's challenges without feeling the effects of stress, anxiety or despair. When you hold the emotional strength to tackle adversity your self-assurance receives a significant boost. You start believing in yourself more, knowing you can handle whatever comes your way.

Nurturing optimism and embracing a growth mindset are closely intertwined with emotional resilience and self-confidence. Optimism is the unwavering belief that, even when faced with challenging situations, things will ultimately turn out for the better. Dogs express this sense of optimism in their daily lives. They're always looking forward to the best, whether it's anticipating playtime or hoping for a treat just around the corner. How does this dog-like optimism reflect in your life and how can you use it to give your self-confidence a boost? The view of a growth mindset is a bit like the adaptable nature of dogs: the belief that your abilities and intelligence can expand and evolve through dedication and hard work. Instead of seeing challenges as daunting roadblocks, people with a growth mindset see them as exciting opportunities for learning and personal growth. How do you view the challenges in your life, and do you think a shift towards a growth mindset could be beneficial for you?

Much like dogs, you can not only face failures head-on but also turn them into stepping-stones that lead to greater self-confidence. Dogs, with their unwavering determination, often encounter challenges and, yes, even setbacks during their adventures, but they don't view these moments as defeats. Instead, they persist and learn from their experiences. How do you typically respond to obstacles and challenges, and can you see the potential for a more dog-like resilience in your approach? It's time for a shift in mindset. Perceived failures aren't signs of inadequacy but instead are building blocks for success. How does this change in perspective feel to you? Can you recall past failures that, on reflection, brought you valuable lessons? It's time to embrace a fresh outlook on challenges and failures, much like dogs do, and feel your self-confidence grow.

We've learned invaluable lessons from our dogs, and we've recognised the significance of self-trust and adaptability in building resilience and have seen how emotional resilience serves as a protective shield, closely linked with self-confidence. Self-reflection is our tool for managing stress and setbacks effectively, while cultivating a positive mindset lets us view every setback as an opportunity for personal growth and a boost to our self-confidence. With these insights in mind, it's time to take action. The exercise ahead acts as part of your overall toolkit with ideas to build your resilience and your path towards unshakable self-confidence.

◆ ◆ ◆

Exercise 1: Setback Analysis

By engaging in this setback analysis and creating a well-defined action plan, you're actively transforming setbacks into opportunities for personal development. This exercise will reinforce your resilience, boost your self-confidence and empower you to navigate future challenges with greater determination and hope.

Instructions

Begin by choosing a recent setback or challenge you've experienced. It could be related to your personal life, work, relationships or any area that holds significance for you. Choose a setback that is recent enough for you to recall the details clearly.

Find a quiet and comfortable space where you can reflect without distractions. Have a notebook or journal, along with a pen or pencil, ready for note-taking.

Take some time to explore the individual factors that caused this setback. Reflect on the circumstances, decisions, actions or external events that played a role. Write down these contributing factors in your notebook.

Next, consider your initial reactions to the setback. Were you frustrated, anxious, sad or angry? Did you experience self-doubt or negative thoughts about your abilities? Write down these initial emotional responses and thoughts.

Now, reevaluate the situation with a fresh perspective. Challenge yourself to find potential lessons and opportunities for personal growth within this setback. Consider what you've learned about yourself, your strengths and areas for improvement. Write down these insights in your notebook.

Based on the lessons and opportunities you've identified, create a practical action plan. Outline specific steps and strategies you can use in the future when faced with similar challenges. Your action plan should be actionable, realistic and tailored to your needs.

Within your action plan, set clear and achievable goals. These goals should reflect how you intend to apply the insights gained from this setback to enhance your resilience and self-confidence. Break down these goals into smaller, manageable steps.

Add time frames to each of the steps within your action plan. Decide when you will begin each step and when you expect to complete them. Having a timeline adds accountability to your plan.

Make a commitment to regularly review and reflect on your progress. Consider scheduling check-ins with yourself to assess how well you're carrying out your action plan and whether any changes are needed.

Put into practice your action plan straight away. Start with the first step and gradually work your way through the goals and timelines you've set. Remember that setbacks are part of the journey, and your newfound resilience will help you face them with confidence.

As you progress, monitor your experiences and adjust your action plan as necessary. Be open to learning from both successes and setbacks along the way.

Celebrate your achievements, no matter how small they may seem. Recognise your growth and acknowledge the effort you've put into enhancing your resilience and self-confidence.

Exercise 2: Cultivating a Positive Mindset

The aim of this exercise is to practice mindfulness. By consistently practicing mindfulness, incorporating positive affirmations and finding silver linings in challenging situations, you'll gradually nurture a positive mindset. This will develop your emotional resilience, allowing you to face adversity with greater confidence and hope, just as dogs do in their daily lives.

Instructions

Choose a specific time each day for this exercise. It can be in the morning, during a lunch break or before bedtime. Consistency is key, so choose a time that suits your routine.

Find a quiet and comfortable place where you can practice mindfulness without disturbances. You can sit or lie down, whichever feels more comfortable for you.

Start by copying the way dogs fully engage with their environment. Close your eyes, take a deep breath and gradually shift your focus to your surroundings. Pay attention to the sounds, smells and sensations around you. Dogs excel at being present in the moment, so try to adopt this same sense of presence.

As you observe your environment, take note of the simple joys and beauty that may often go unnoticed. Dogs find happiness in the smallest things. Reflect on these small pleasures and find appreciation in them.

Consider adding positive affirmations into your daily routine. These are short, positive statements that reinforce a more optimistic mindset. For example, you can say, 'I am capable of handling challenges,' or 'I find opportunities for growth in every situation.' Repeat these affirmations to yourself during your mindfulness practice.

When you encounter a challenging situation during your day, try to find a silver lining or growth opportunity within it. Dogs have a natural ability to adapt and find joy even in adversity. Copy this by reframing difficulties as chances to learn and evolve.

Commit to this exercise daily, even if it's just for a few minutes. Consistent practice will gradually strengthen your mindfulness skills and positive mindset.

Consider keeping a journal to document your daily observations and reflections. Note any shifts in your mindset or any newfound appreciation for the simple joys around you. This journal can serve as a record of your progress and a source of inspiration.

If you feel comfortable, share your experiences and insights with a friend or loved one. Engaging in discussions about your journey to cultivate a positive mindset can reinforce your commitment to this practice.

Remember that developing a positive mindset is a gradual process. Like dogs, you can learn to embrace each moment with optimism and trust that challenges hold opportunities for growth.

Exercise 3: Stress Management Toolkit

Creating and regularly using a personalised stress management toolkit will help you to effectively navigate stress and difficulties. This toolkit becomes a valuable resource for maintaining emotional resilience and boosting self-confidence, helping you face life's challenges with greater assurance.

Instructions

Begin by building a list of stress management techniques that resonate with you. Consider the coping mechanisms of dogs as your inspiration. Techniques may include exercise, meditation, engaging in hobbies, seeking social support, practicing mindfulness or any other strategies that help you relax and de-stress.

Review your list of stress management techniques and select the ones that you find most appealing and suitable for your lifestyle. Remember that everyone is different, so choose techniques that align with your preferences and needs. These should be activities that you genuinely enjoy and can easily incorporate into your daily life.

Assemble the tools and resources needed for each stress management technique you've chosen. For example, if exercise is one of your chosen techniques, ensure you have comfortable workout attire, a yoga mat or any exercise equipment you prefer. If meditation is on your list, consider creating a designated meditation space with calming decorations or cushions.

Over the course of several weeks, experiment with the stress management techniques in your toolkit. Start with one or two techniques and gradually incorporate others. Pay attention to how each technique makes you feel and its effectiveness in reducing stress and increasing your emotional resilience.

Keep a stress management journal to document your experiences. Write about the techniques you tried, how they impacted your mood and stress levels, and any insights or observations you made. Note which techniques resonate with you the most and which ones you'd like to continue using.

Don't hesitate to share your stress management journey with friends, family members or support groups. Discuss your experiences and learn from others who may have additional insights or techniques to share. Social support can enhance the effectiveness of your stress management toolkit.

As you continue to experiment with stress management techniques, be open to changing your toolkit. If you discover new techniques that work well for you, add them to your toolkit. Likewise, if you find that certain techniques are less effective, consider replacing them with others that better suit your needs.

Make stress management a regular part of your routine. Dedicate time each day or week to engage in the techniques from your toolkit. Consistent practice will reinforce your emotional resilience and boost your self-confidence.

Recognise that stressors and challenges may change over time. Be prepared to adapt your stress management toolkit to address new situations or sources of stress that may arise.

Acknowledge and celebrate your progress in managing stress and building emotional resilience. Recognise the positive impact this has on your self-confidence and overall well-being.

CHAPTER 4: LOYALTY

Practising the art of self-loyalty can powerfully boost your self-esteem and confidence. Have you ever thought about how your dog's loyalty mirrors the idea of being loyal to yourself? How does the trust and devotion your dog shows you connect with your relationship with your own inner self? When we think of loyalty, our dogs often take centre stage as the prime example. They are renowned for their unwavering dedication to their humans. What makes their loyalty so special? It's not just about attachment; it's about trust, understanding and that unbreakable bond founded on pure, unconditional love. This same loyalty, the kind we admire in our dogs, can be the secret for boosting your self-confidence and self-worth. Just as dogs pledge their allegiance to us, self-loyalty is the foundation for your self-esteem and self-value. It's about having your own back, recognising your inherent worth and being your own unwavering supporter through life's twists and turns. Picture this: you treat yourself with the same care, respect, and kindness that you shower upon your dog. Isn't that a lovely thought?

Dogs never try to be something they're not. They're themselves, no matter the situation, and they do it without a hint of apology. Adopting self-loyalty reinforces the idea that you deserve your unwavering support and acceptance. It's a declaration to yourself that you are valuable just as you are, without the need to conform to external standards or pretend to be someone you're not. Being authentic means you're not donning masks or disguises to fit into someone else's idea of who or what you should be. It's about living in harmony with your values, beliefs and dreams and making choices that resonate with your true self. When you truly embrace your authentic self, you're essentially giving yourself a badge of self-loyalty. It's a declaration that you are deserving of your own unwavering support and love, just the way you are.

Another important aspect of self-loyalty revolves around respecting your boundaries and recognizing your needs. How often do you set clear boundaries in your life, whether it's in your relationships, at work or even in your personal space? Are your boundaries serving you well or could they use some adjustment? What are your most pressing needs right now, and how might addressing them boost your sense of self-commitment? And when it comes to your needs, are you as attentive to them as you are to dog's needs? Setting and maintaining healthy boundaries is like building a protective fortress around your self-worth and emotional well-being. It's a vital act of self-loyalty that safeguards your confidence.

Dogs, with their intuitive understanding of personal space and their keen sense of what they require, offer valuable lessons in this regard. Just as dogs understand when they need rest, play, or affection and aren't afraid to communicate those needs, you too can benefit from identifying and prioritising your personal boundaries and needs. Setting and maintaining healthy boundaries is a powerful act of self-loyalty. It's about establishing the limits of what you're willing to accept or tolerate in your relationships, work and life in general. By doing so, you create a protective barrier that shields your emotional well-being and self-esteem. Prioritising your needs is an extension of self-loyalty. It involves recognising that your emotional, physical and psychological well-being are paramount. Just as you would ensure your dog has access to food, water and exercise, you must acknowledge and address your own needs. Whether it's the need for self-care, personal growth or simply time for relaxation, honouring these needs is a testament to your self-commitment.

When we think about loyalty, it's not just about unwavering commitment; it's also about kindness and understanding. Dogs excel in this aspect, showering their humans with affection and support. They have an incredible knack for sensing when we're feeling down, offering comfort without judgement. In the realm of self-loyalty, self-compassion plays a similar role. It's the gentle, understanding and loving treatment we offer ourselves. Self-compassion is a crucial element of self-loyalty. It involves recognising your own suffering or imperfections and responding to them with the same kindness and care that you would extend to a special friend. How often do you offer kindness and understanding to yourself? Self-compassion encourages you to be understanding and forgiving towards yourself, especially during times of difficulty or self-doubt. It's that soothing voice within, reassuring you that it's okay to stumble and that you're deserving of love and understanding, especially when self-doubt creeps in. Do you find it easier to extend compassion to others than to yourself? How might your self-esteem and self-confidence benefit from embracing self-compassion as a daily practice? By learning from the compassion that dogs offer, you'll be better equipped to cultivate a nurturing and loyal relationship with yourself, ultimately bolstering your self-confidence.

Dogs don't go around seeking approval or validation from others to know their worth. They possess an innate sense of self-value. Now, reflect on your own life. How often do you find yourself craving validation from external sources, perhaps from friends, family or social media? What if you could embrace the power of self-validation, recognising that your worth doesn't depend on others' opinions? In the world of humans, self-loyalty often results in recognising and embracing the power of self-validation. This means understanding that your worth and value come from within, not from the opinions or judgements of others. Self-validation is the act of acknowledging your own feelings, thoughts and experiences as valid and legitimate. It's about trusting your own judgement and intuition. Dogs trust their instincts, and they don't second-guess their feelings; they simply feel and respond authentically. Similarly, self-validation encourages you to honour your emotions, beliefs and choices without seeking constant approval or validation from others. How might your life change if you learned to trust your inner compass more and seek external validation less?

In the exploration of self-loyalty, we've uncovered insights that can reshape our relationship with ourselves. Much like the unwavering loyalty dogs demonstrate, self-loyalty holds the key to boosting self-esteem and self-confidence. It urges us to treat ourselves with the same care, kindness and respect we lavish upon our dogs. Authenticity encourages us to embrace our true selves without pretence. Setting and respecting boundaries, prioritising our needs, extending self-compassion and embracing self-validation all contribute to the journey of self-loyalty. As we draw inspiration from our dogs' unwavering trust and devotion, we discover that self-loyalty is not just a lesson from them but a precious gift we give ourselves on the path to unwavering self-assurance. So, consider how these lessons might reshape your self-relationship, and remember that, like your loyal dog, you too deserve your own unwavering devotion and love. The following exercises will add to your toolbox of resources that lead towards unshakable confidence.

Exercise 1: Mirror of Self-Compassion

The aim of this exercise is to develop self-compassion by treating yourself with the same kindness, understanding and care that you would extend to a special friend. By practicing self-compassion in front of a mirror, you can reinforce a positive self-image and strengthen your sense of self-loyalty, ultimately boosting your self-esteem and self-confidence.

Instructions

Choose a quiet and private space where you feel comfortable and won't be interrupted. This exercise requires your full attention and focus.

Position yourself in front of a mirror so that you can see your reflection clearly. It can be a full-length mirror or one that shows your face and upper body.

Begin by taking a few slow and deep breaths to calm your mind and centre yourself. Inhale deeply through your nose, hold for a few seconds and exhale slowly through your mouth.

Gaze into your own eyes in the mirror. Maintain eye contact with yourself throughout the exercise. This may feel challenging at first, but it's essential for the exercise's effectiveness.

Start speaking to yourself with the same level of compassion and understanding that you would offer to a close friend. Use affirming words and gestures to convey your support and care. For example, say soothing and encouraging statements like, 'I am worthy of love and compassion,' 'I accept myself just as I am,' or 'I am deserving of kindness.'

Use gentle and reassuring body language, such as smiling at yourself or placing your hand over your heart.

Avoid self-criticism, judgement or negative self-talk during this exercise. If any negative thoughts arise, acknowledge them and then refocus on the positive affirmations.

Continue to express love, understanding and self-compassion for several minutes. Allow the feelings of self-love and self-loyalty to wash over you.

If you encounter areas of self-doubt or discomfort during the exercise, acknowledge them with kindness. Remember that imperfections are part of being human and can be opportunities for growth and self-compassion.

After the exercise, take a few moments to reflect on your experience. Consider any emotions or insights that came up during the practice. You may choose to journal your thoughts and feelings for greater self-awareness.

This exercise can be repeated as often as you like, ideally incorporating it into your daily routine. The more you practice self-compassion in front of the mirror, the more it becomes a natural part of your self-loyalty journey.

Exercise 2: Boundaries and You

The aim of this exercise is to help you identify, establish or adjust your personal boundaries, both physical and emotional. By carrying out the exercise you can gain understanding around your physical and emotional boundaries, and this empowers you to take control of your personal space and emotional well-being, ultimately contributing to your overall sense of self-assurance.

Instructions

Choose a quiet and comfortable space where you can engage in thoughtful reflection without distractions. Have a notebook or journal and a pen or pencil ready for writing down your thoughts and boundaries.

Start by considering your physical boundaries. These include your personal space, comfort zones and physical limits. Reflect on how comfortable you are with physical touch, hugging or close contact with others. Ask yourself questions like:

'What makes me feel physically comfortable or uncomfortable around others?'

'Do I have any physical boundaries that I need to communicate or enforce?'

'How do my physical boundaries contribute to my well-being?'

Move on to your emotional boundaries. These relate to your feelings, emotions and emotional space. Think about how you handle emotions, both yours and others. Consider questions such as:

'What emotions do I find challenging to share or express with others?'

'Are there situations or topics that make me feel emotionally vulnerable?'

'Do I need to establish emotional boundaries to protect my emotional well-being?'

In your journal create two lists: one for your physical boundaries and another for your emotional boundaries. Write down specific boundaries that you have identified or need to set. Be as detailed as possible. For example:

Physical Boundaries List
'I need personal space when I work or study.'
'I am uncomfortable with unsolicited physical touch.'
'I need time alone to recharge.'

Emotional Boundaries List
'I am selective about sharing personal feelings with acquaintances.'
'I don't want to engage in discussions about my past traumas with certain people.'
'I need to establish boundaries around my availability for emotional support.'

Review your lists of physical and emotional boundaries. Consider whether there are any changes you need to make. Are there boundaries you haven't been respecting or ones you should communicate more clearly to others?

Think about how these changes could positively impact your self-commitment and overall well-being.

Take a moment to visualise how respecting and maintaining these boundaries can improve your self-commitment and self-loyalty. Imagine yourself confidently asserting your boundaries and experiencing a greater sense of emotional well-being as a result.

Write in your journal about your insights and reflections during this exercise. Note any challenges you anticipate in setting or adjusting boundaries and how you plan to overcome them.

Based on your reflections, create an action plan for implementing and communicating your boundaries. Include steps for asserting your boundaries respectfully and effectively.

Reinforce the idea that respecting your boundaries is an act of self-loyalty. Make a commitment to yourself to prioritise and maintain these boundaries to safeguard your well-being and enhance your self-esteem and self-confidence.

As you grow and change, your boundaries may evolve so revisit your lists of boundaries regularly and decide whether any adjustments are needed.

Exercise 3: Mirror of Authenticity

Through this exercise you can develop a deeper understanding of how authenticity influences your self-loyalty and self-confidence. By identifying areas where you may not fully embrace your authentic self and taking steps towards greater alignment with your values and beliefs, you can enhance your self-assurance.

Instructions

Choose a quiet, comfortable space where you can focus on self-reflection without distractions. Have a notebook or journal and a pen or pencil ready for writing down your thoughts and reflections.

Begin by reflecting on your life and identifying areas where you may be wearing masks or not fully embracing your authentic self. Consider aspects of your life, such as work, relationships or personal goals, where you may be conforming to external expectations or suppressing your true values and beliefs.

Ask yourself questions such as:

'In what situations do I feel like I'm not being my authentic self?'

'Are there roles or personas I've adopted to fit in or please others?'

'How do these inauthentic behaviours affect my self-loyalty and self-confidence?'

In your journal create a list of authenticity goals or actions you can take to align your actions more closely with your true values and beliefs. Be specific and actionable in your goals. For example:

'Practice open communication in my relationship with (name) by sharing my true feelings and thoughts.'

'Express my creative side by dedicating time to pursue (hobby/ passion).'

'At work, be honest about my strengths and weaknesses, and stop pretending to know everything.'

Select one aspect of your life from the list of authenticity goals to focus on initially. Choose an area where practicing authenticity feels manageable and relevant to your current circumstances.

Practice authenticity by aligning your actions, words and decisions with your true values and beliefs in that particular area of your life. Be conscious of your thoughts and behaviours, and make an effort to be genuine and true to yourself.

After some time has passed (this could be a week or more, depending on your chosen aspect), reflect on the impact of practicing authenticity. Consider how this change has influenced your self-loyalty and self-confidence. Ask yourself questions like:

'How did it feel to practice authenticity in this aspect of my life?'

'Did I experience any challenges or resistance?'

'How did others respond to my authentic self?'

'Do I notice any changes in my self-loyalty and self-confidence?'

Write in your journal about your observations and experiences during this process. Write down any insights or shifts in your self-loyalty and self-confidence that you've noticed as a result of practicing authenticity.

Based on your reflections and observations, set new authenticity goals or continue working on the initial one. Consider applying authenticity to different areas of your life to further enhance your self-loyalty and self-confidence.

Make self-reflection and the practice of authenticity an ongoing part of your personal growth journey. Regularly revisit and expand your authenticity goals to align more aspects of your life with your authentic self, reinforcing your self-loyalty and self-confidence over time.

CHAPTER 5: PLAYFULNESS

Dogs possess an incredible talent for discovering joy in the simplest of things. Whether they're chasing a ball or playing in the park, their happiness in the moment always has the ability to bring a smile to our faces. Their playful spirit is pure magic. For dogs, playfulness is an expression of their passion for life. It's as if they're sending us a message, saying, 'Hey, let's enjoy the moment!' What is it about playfulness that makes it such a strong source of positivity? Their ability to live fully in the present, absorbed in play, serves as an important reminder that playfulness isn't just about having fun; it's a reflection of inner contentment and self-assurance.

Dogs seem to navigate life with a free spirit. Have you ever noticed their ability to embrace each moment with enthusiasm and freedom? It's wonderful to witness how their playfulness forms the foundation of their self-confidence. Can you recall a specific moment when your dog's playfulness inspired you or made you feel more confident? Their playful antics offer a valuable lesson, and that playfulness isn't just about fun and games; it's an important source of inner security and happiness. What do you think lies at the heart of the connection between playfulness and self-esteem?

Playfulness, often associated with childhood and carefree moments, is a state of mind that goes above age and circumstances. Have you ever wondered why playfulness holds such a special place in our hearts, regardless of our age? It's characterised by a deep sense of joy, freedom and creativity.

When we tap into our playful selves, we embrace the world with a childlike wonder, freed from the weight of adulthood. How does embracing playfulness make you feel? Playfulness is not a frivolous indulgence; it's a powerful force that contributes significantly to enhancing confidence. At its core, playfulness allows us to break free from the constraints of self-doubt and inhibition. It encourages us to let go of our fears, to be unapologetically ourselves and to express our authenticity without reservation. How do you think playfulness can help you embrace your true self? When we infuse our lives with playfulness, we create an environment in which confidence can flourish.

Childhood is a time when playfulness flows naturally, and the world is seen through the lens of wonder and curiosity. What are your fondest memories of childhood play? Think back to the times when you ran through the grass, climbed trees or played make-believe with friends. These moments were not just about having fun; they were a vital part of your development. They allowed you to explore your imagination, build social skills and, most importantly, foster a sense of confidence in your abilities. You were not afraid to try new things, to fail and to learn from those failures because you approached life with a playful spirit. However, as we grow older and assume more responsibilities, the transition from childhood playfulness to adulthood often leads to a decline in our willingness to embrace play. Has adulthood impacted your willingness to be playful?

The weight of adulthood can curb our sense of spontaneity and creativity, and as a result, our confidence can wane. We become more cautious, fearing the judgement of others and the consequences of taking risks. How can we rediscover and nurture our playful spirit in the midst of our adult responsibilities? Reflecting on this transition isn't about dwelling in nostalgia for the past; it's about recognising the profound influence childhood playfulness had on our confidence. Have you ever thought about how those carefree moments shaped who you are today? It serves as a reminder that the ability to be playful is still within us, waiting to be rekindled. How do you feel about the idea of reigniting your playful spirit? By reintroducing elements of playfulness into our lives, we can bridge the gap between the carefree confidence of childhood and the responsibilities of adulthood. In doing so, we unlock the potential for greater self-assurance and happiness in our present lives.

While playfulness offers clear benefits, many of us struggle to let loose their inner playful spirit fully. Can you relate to this? Recognising the barriers to playfulness is a crucial step on our path to greater confidence and happiness. As we age, social expectations and the weight of responsibilities can stifle our playful side, creating the fear of appearing childish or irresponsible. The hectic pace of life often leaves us with little time or energy for playfulness, especially when stress and anxiety narrow our perspective. Self-criticism and perfectionism frequently act as barriers to our playful nature, making us hesitant to embrace imperfection and take risks. Can you recall a time when you hesitated to engage in something fun because of a fear of making mistakes?

Vulnerability is at the heart of playfulness yet, as adults, we often build walls to protect ourselves from judgement or appearing foolish. Have you ever held back from being playful because you are worried about what others might think? It's a common concern and can delay our journey to embracing playfulness. Let's talk about time, or the lack of it. Modern life can feel like a relentless sprint, can't it? Work, family and all those responsibilities, they pile up, leaving us with the feeling that there's simply no room for play. It's like time becomes this elusive thing that slips through our fingers, and we're left with the impression that we can't afford to be playful.

You know, one of the most powerful steps on this journey to rediscover your playful self is simply giving yourself permission to play. It's like granting yourself a precious gift in a world that often tells us to be serious and productive all the time. It's not just okay for adults to make time for playfulness, it's actually incredibly good for us. It's a reminder that maturity doesn't mean we have to let go of joy and spontaneity. So, what if we made a pact right now to let ourselves play without any guilt or self-criticism? Can you imagine the positive impact it could have on your confidence and overall well-being? Understanding the connection between playfulness and confidence is important to truly accepting the transformation that adding more play to your life can bring. Playfulness isn't just about having a good time; it's like a secret ingredient that supercharges your self-esteem and bolsters your confidence. Every time you engage in a playful activity and experience those moments of joy and achievement, you're actually building up your self-worth and self-esteem.

It's not just a feeling, as science backs up the strong connection between playfulness and confidence. Researchers have examined this and found some fascinating results. When you engage in playful activities, your brain releases endorphins, those magical mood boosters. These endorphins not only make you happier but also help lower stress levels, creating a perfect environment for confidence to flourish. Your brain's reward system lights up during play, reinforcing that positive link between playfulness and self-esteem.

When you embrace playfulness you're also opening the door to a growth mindset. This mindset is all about believing that your abilities and intelligence can expand through dedication and effort. It's like a mental switch that flips when you play. You become more willing to make mistakes, take calculated risks and see failures as valuable lessons rather than blows to your self-esteem. This shift in mindset is like a secret weapon for boosting your confidence because it transforms challenges from daunting threats to exciting chances for personal growth. Can you recall a time when playfulness helped you see a challenge in a new light? How did it impact your confidence in tackling similar obstacles in the future?

Playfulness and mindfulness share the ability to immerse you in the present moment, offering a shield against stress and worry. Engaging in playful activities reduces mental clutter, lowers stress levels and refreshes your perspective, all of which contribute to heightened self-assuredness. Also, playful movement helps release physical tension and promotes relaxation, creating a confident presence. Playful social interactions strengthen bonds and foster a sense of belonging, boosting social confidence. Using play as a stress-relief tool empowers you to intentionally incorporate it into your daily routine, enhancing confidence and resilience. How can you bring more playfulness into your life as a stress-relief strategy, and when have playful activities helped you manage stress effectively?

Playfulness isn't limited to personal growth; it's also a powerful tool for building and nurturing relationships. Whether with friends, family or romantic partners, introducing playfulness into your interactions can strengthen connections and enhance the quality of your relationships. Integrating playfulness into your relationships can foster trust, laughter and shared joy. It breaks down barriers, encourages open communication and creates a sense of playfulness in your social circles. How do you currently incorporate playfulness into your relationships? Can you recall a moment when playfulness enhanced your connection with someone? By prioritising play in your interactions, you'll not only deepen your connections but also contribute to the development of a more playful and confident version of yourself.

Playfulness, as demonstrated by dogs, serves as a reminder that playfulness rises above age and circumstances, offering a gateway to joy, spontaneity and creativity. Understanding and overcoming the barriers that often stifle our playful spirits such as social expectations, life's demands, self-judgement, fear of vulnerability and perceived time constraints is the first step towards greater confidence and happiness. Playfulness extends beyond personal growth; it enriches our relationships, fostering trust, laughter and shared moments of joy. By prioritising playfulness in our interactions, we not only strengthen our bonds but also cultivate a more playful and confident self. So, let's reintroduce playfulness into our lives, bridging the gap between childhood's carefree confidence and the responsibilities of adulthood, unlocking the potential for greater self-assurance and happiness in the process. The following exercises will help you develop your playful spirit.

Exercise 1: Embracing Playfulness

The aim of this exercise is to cultivate and experience the joy of playfulness in your daily life, much like your canine companion. By letting go of inhibitions and trying new activities, you'll enhance your self-esteem and confidence.

Instructions

Choose an activity or hobby that genuinely brings you joy. It could be something you used to enjoy but haven't done in a while or something completely new. This could be as simple as dancing, drawing, playing a musical instrument, cooking or trying a new sport.

Set the stage for playfulness by creating an environment that encourages free expression. Clear your space of distractions and create a mood that suits your chosen activity. For instance, if you're going to dance, put on your favourite music and dim the lights to create an enjoyable atmosphere.

Playfulness thrives when you let go of the need to be perfect. Understand that it's perfectly okay not to be the best at this activity immediately. The focus is on the experience, joy and learning rather than achieving perfection. Embrace imperfection as a part of the process.

Push your boundaries by trying new things within your chosen activity. If you're playing a musical instrument, attempt a new song or technique you've never tried. In sports, challenge yourself with a new move or exercise. By stepping out of your comfort zone you'll experience the thrill of adventure and personal growth.

While doing the activity focus on being fully present in the moment. Don't let distracting thoughts or worries about the past or future creep in. The goal is to experience the activity with undivided attention, just like your dog is fully absorbed in play.

Regardless of the outcome, celebrate your efforts and the enjoyment you get from the activity. Whether you're learning a new chord on a guitar or attempting a new recipe, acknowledge the progress you're making and the happiness it brings.

Continue to practice playfulness in various aspects of your life. Try new activities or revisit those that bring you joy. The more you infuse playfulness into your routine, the more confident and self-assured you'll become.

After each playfulness session take a moment to reflect on how it made you feel. Did you experience a sense of joy and spontaneity? How did embracing imperfection impact your mindset? Reflecting on these experiences will help you recognise the link between playfulness and your confidence.

Share your journey towards embracing playfulness with friends or loved ones. Encourage them to join you in embracing playfulness and building self-esteem together.

◆ ◆ ◆

Exercise 2: Overcoming Barriers to Playfulness

This exercise aims to help you identify and overcome the common barriers that stifle your playfulness. By recognising and actively addressing these barriers, you'll create space for playfulness in your life, which will lead to greater self-confidence and happiness. Overcoming these obstacles is a transformative journey that bridges the gap between the carefree confidence of childhood and the responsibilities of adulthood, unlocking the potential for a more confident and joyful self.

Instructions

Begin by reflecting on your own life and circumstances. Take a moment to identify the barriers that have, at times, held back your ability to embrace playfulness. These may include general expectations, self-judgement and perceived time constraints. Consider specific instances where these barriers showed up in your life.

Dive deeper into the impact of social expectations on your willingness to be playful. How have cultural norms or social pressures influenced your choices and behaviours? Reflect on whether you've ever felt judged for being playful or carefree in an environment that prioritises seriousness.

Challenge the societal norms that discourage playfulness. Remind yourself that it's perfectly acceptable for adults to embrace play and joy. Explore environments or communities that celebrate playfulness.

Consider the role of self-judgement and perfectionism in suppressing your playful spirit. Have you ever hesitated to engage in playful activities due to concerns about appearing foolish or making mistakes? Reflect on how the fear of imperfection has held you back.

Replace self-judgement with self-compassion. Understand that it's okay to make mistakes and be imperfect. When you feel self-critical, counter it with kind and encouraging self-talk.

Think about the role of time-related barriers in your life. How often have you felt that the demands and responsibilities of adulthood leave you with little room for playfulness? Reflect on moments when you felt overwhelmed or too busy to engage in playful activities.

Reevaluate how you manage your time and prioritise activities. Look for opportunities to include playfulness in your schedule. This might involve setting aside specific time for hobbies, leisure or simply being spontaneous.

Surround yourself with individuals who encourage and appreciate your playful side. Share your desire to be more playful with friends and family, and ask for their support in making room for play in your life.

Embrace mindfulness practices to alleviate stress and create mental space for playfulness. Techniques like meditation and deep breathing can help you stay present in the moment and free your mind from anxieties.

Gradually reintroduce playfulness into your life. Start with small, manageable steps and gradually expand your playful activities. Track how these activities make you feel and the positive impact on your confidence.

Incorporate regular self-reflection into your routine to monitor your progress in overcoming these barriers. Celebrate the moments when you successfully push past these obstacles and enjoy playful experiences.

Share your journey of overcoming barriers to playfulness with friends or loved ones who may be experiencing similar challenges. Encourage them to identify and address their barriers, fostering a supportive community for enhancing self-confidence.

By recognising and actively addressing these barriers, you'll create space for playfulness in your life, which will lead to greater self-confidence and happiness. Overcoming these obstacles is a transformative journey that bridges the gap between the carefree confidence of childhood and the responsibilities of adulthood, unlocking the potential for a more confident and joyful self.

Exercise 3: Playfulness as a Stress-Relief Strategy

The aim of this exercise is to help you incorporate playfulness into your life intentionally as a stress management strategy. By identifying and engaging in playful activities that help you alleviate stress and rejuvenate your perspective, you can enhance your overall well-being and boost your self-confidence.

Instructions

Begin by reflecting on the sources of stress in your life. Take a moment to identify the situations, responsibilities or triggers that often lead to stress and anxiety. Understand how stress affects your mood, outlook and self-confidence.

Consider the activities or moments in your life that have, in the past, helped you manage stress effectively. These can be moments of playfulness, fun or relaxation that brought relief from stress. Examples might include engaging in a hobby, playing with pets, dancing, singing or participating in creative activities.

Create a list of these stress-relief activities. Write down as many as you can think of, whether they involve physical movement, creative expression or simply letting loose. Having a variety of options will be useful for different situations and stress levels.

Develop a practice of being aware of your stress levels throughout the day. Notice when you're starting to feel stressed or overwhelmed. This self-awareness will help you proactively address stress with playfulness.

When you recognise stress building up, choose one of the stress-relief activities from your list and incorporate it into your routine. This could be a short dance break, a brief moment of play with your pet or engaging in a creative outlet. Engage in these stress-relief activities with full presence in the moment. Let go of worries and focus entirely on the joy and relaxation the activity brings.

Pay attention to how engaging in these playful activities affects your stress levels. Take note of any changes in your mood, tension and overall well-being. Reflect on how these moments of playfulness impact your self-confidence.

Incorporate playful stress-relief activities into your daily or weekly routine. Designate specific times for these activities, especially during periods when you anticipate higher stress levels, like work deadlines or personal challenges.

Encourage friends, family members or coworkers to join you in playful stress-relief activities. Sharing these moments of playfulness with others can create a supportive and fun environment, enhancing your social connections and sense of belonging.

Keep a journal where you document your experiences with playfulness as a stress-relief strategy. Note which activities were the most effective and how they influenced your self-confidence. Track your progress in managing stress through playfulness.

CHAPTER 6: PATIENCE

The roots of dogs' patience run deep, fed by their unconditional love, unwavering loyalty, contentment in the present, forgiveness and their commitment to learning and growing. They are masters at valuing the present moment, finding happiness in life's simplest pleasures without constantly craving more. They demonstrate incredible patience with their ability to accept the present circumstances. They are also tolerant and forgiving. They don't hold on to grudges; instead, they are quick to let go of past wrongs. This forgiving nature leads to understanding empathy and the chance for growth and reconciliation within our relationships.

Have you ever admired how dogs handle unexpected situations? A failed catch in a game of fetch or a sudden change in routine doesn't deter them. They carry on with enthusiasm and a positive outlook, teaching us to confront life's surprises with grace and determination. Dogs are also masters of unwavering love and support, especially on our tough days. They sense our moods and respond with empathy, reminding us that patience involves being compassionate to ourselves during challenges. They shine at living in the present, appreciating life's small joys. Whether it's a gentle belly rub or a long walk, they demonstrate patience that encourages us to fully embrace the present moment rather than rushing forward. We often find ourselves facing choices that require patience, whether it's pursuing long-term goals or navigating through life's challenges. It's not merely about waiting; it's about believing in the process, staying committed even when things get tough, and having confidence in the rewards that come from dedication and persistence. Can these dog-inspired lessons help you approach life's challenges with more patience and optimism? How might their ability to value the present inspire you to find joy in life's simple pleasures?

Patience is all about keeping your cool when life throws surprises your way. It's that enduring quality, especially when the going gets tough, and this endurance plays an important role in nurturing your self-belief and self-esteem. When you choose patience, you're stating, 'I'm committed to my goals, and I've got the confidence to tackle any obstacles that may come up.' Psychological research supports this idea. Patient individuals often show higher levels of self-control, which, in turn, leads to a boost in self-esteem and self-belief. When you approach your goals with patience, you're more inclined to persist, even when life throws you some unexpected challenges. This persistence builds something known as self-efficacy, which means believing in yourself to overcome hurdles and achieve your dreams, a fundamental part of confidence.

Patience often walks hand in hand with self-reflection and mindfulness. It's like shining a light on your inner self, digging into your values and building a deeper connection with your goals. This journey of self-discovery allows you to match your actions with your authentic self. And the result? A significant boost in self-belief and self-esteem. So, have you ever contemplated the role of patience in your personal journey? Which of your goals or challenges might benefit from a touch more patience? How could aligning your actions with your true self positively influence your self-belief and self-esteem? It's all about striking that balance between determination and self-assuredness.

Patience is a useful companion in our lives. It reveals itself in various forms, from the patience to be an attentive listener to the patience needed to take on challenges or chase long-term ambitions and dreams. Every bit of patience in your daily life adds another layer to your self-esteem, supporting you to handle life's surprises with skill and confidence. Real-life stories are full of people who've harnessed the power of patience to raise their self-esteem. Look at entrepreneurs, for example. They're out there establishing thriving businesses, and the common thread among them? They've continued through countless setbacks and problems with patience. It's not just about business success; it's about possessing unwavering confidence in their own abilities. Then there are those embarking on journeys towards weight loss and healthier lifestyles. Patience serves as their secret ingredient. They make consistent progress, resulting in a total transformation of their self-esteem and body image. Do you have real-life heroes in your life who've used patience as a way to turbocharge their self-esteem?

Conquering impatience and frustration is an important step on your journey to building self-esteem and confidence. Uncontrolled impatience often paves the way for stress, anxiety and good old self-doubt. How do you react when frustration pays you a visit? Have you ever thought about exploring the practice of mindfulness? It can be really effective. Picture this: you're fully immersed in the present moment, devoid of judgement. That's the essence of mindfulness. So, when those feelings of impatience start popping up what's your go-to move? It's simple. Take a deep breath and acknowledge those feelings without judgement. It's similar to applying a secret weapon that empowers you with greater control over your emotions and responses.

Now, let's shift our focus to resilience and how it can help cultivate patience, confidence and self-esteem. What exactly is resilience? As we have read in a previous chapter, it's the remarkable ability to bounce back from life's unexpected setbacks. Resilience teaches us that failure isn't the final destination; it's merely a rest area on your journey towards growth. How do you usually respond to the challenges and setbacks that life throws your way? Do they tend to fan the flames of impatience and frustration, or do you welcome them as invaluable learning experiences and stepping-stones towards self-improvement? The more resilient you grow, the less these hurdles will disrupt your balance of patience and your level of confidence.

Dogs teach us that patience is necessary for nurturing self-belief and resilience. Become your own unwavering advocate and shower yourself with self-compassion, particularly when impatience leads to self-criticism. Keep in mind, perfection is an illusion, and the bumps along the road are simply part and parcel of life's journey. By incorporating these tactics into your daily routine and taming impatience and frustration, you'll find yourself well-prepared to build your self-esteem and confidence. Over time, you'll grow into a more resilient, self-assured version of yourself, enjoying a sense of well-being and solid self-belief. Yet, knowing all this is merely the start. The real magic starts when you put it into practice, which is why the exercises that follow are important. They are designed to help you apply these insights to your life to help build your patience muscles.

Exercise 1: Embrace Delayed Gratification

The aim of this exercise is to develop patience by learning to resist immediate rewards and wait for more significant, long-term benefits. By embracing delayed gratification you can learn to resist the allure of immediate rewards and develop the patience needed to pursue long-term objectives with confidence.

Instructions

Begin by clearly defining your long-term objectives. These could be related to your career, personal growth or any other area of your life where patience is essential.

Divide your long-term goals into smaller, manageable milestones. This will make the journey more achievable and allow you to track your progress.

Develop a visual representation of your long-term goals and the steps needed to achieve them. This could be a timeline, vision board or a written plan.

Incorporate daily or weekly routines that require patience. For example, if your goal is to save money, start by setting a portion of your income aside and let it build up over time.

Pay attention to moments when you feel impatient and are tempted by immediate rewards or shortcuts. Acknowledge these feelings without judgement.

Remind yourself of the long-term benefits of your goals. Repeat your commitment to the process and understand that waiting for a bigger reward will be worth it.

As you reach the smaller milestones take time to celebrate your progress. This will motivate you to continue on your patient journey.

Keep a journal or record of your progress. Note how your patience is helping you stay committed and confident in achieving your long-term goals.

Maintain a positive mindset. Focus on the personal growth and lessons gained during your journey. Remind yourself that patience is a valuable skill that builds self-belief.

Exercise 2: Stay Present in the Moment

Cultivate patience with this exercise by learning to appreciate and immerse yourself in the present moment, just as dogs do.

Instructions

Start with a simple breathing exercise. Find a quiet space, sit or lie down comfortably, and take a few deep, conscious breaths. Inhale deeply through your nose, hold for a moment, and exhale slowly through your mouth. Focus your attention entirely on your breath, letting go of other thoughts. This helps you anchor yourself in the present.

Spend time each day observing your surroundings, even if you're in a familiar environment. Take in the details, colours and textures. Challenge yourself to notice things you might usually overlook.

Consciously engage your senses throughout the day. When you eat, relish each bite by paying attention to the flavours, textures and smells. Touch objects with awareness to feel their surfaces. Listen to sounds around you, both near and far.

Mimic dogs by finding joy in simple pleasures. Take time to relish the warmth of the sun on your skin, enjoy a favourite meal or appreciate a gentle breeze. Fully engage in these experiences, leaving no room for distractions.

Maintain a gratitude journal or take a few minutes each day to reflect on the things you're grateful for in your life. This practice encourages appreciation for the present moment.

Recognise when you're rushing from one task or thought to the next. When this happens, pause and remind yourself to slow down and be present. Avoid constant planning for what's next.

Allocate specific periods each day to disconnect from electronic devices. Use this time to connect with the world around you, engage in conversations or immerse yourself in nature.

Take mindful walks where you pay attention to every step, sensation and breath. Leave behind any distractions, like headphones or the need to reach a destination quickly.

Regularly reflect on your journey to staying present in the moment. Notice how you're becoming more patient and appreciative of your experiences. Acknowledge the benefits of this practice in your overall well-being and self-belief.

Exercise 3: Endure Setbacks with Grace

This exercise will help you develop patience through resilience and a positive outlook when facing challenges. It will build the mindset that views setbacks as opportunities for growth and learning and encourage you to approach adversity with determination and confidence, ultimately reinforcing your self-belief.

Instructions

When faced with a setback, start by acknowledging your

emotions. It's natural to feel disappointment, frustration or sadness. Give yourself a moment to feel these emotions without judgement.

Challenge your initial negative reactions by reframing your perspective. Instead of viewing a setback as a failure, see it as an opportunity for growth and learning. Understand that many successful people have faced setbacks on their path to achievement.

Examine your expectations to ensure they are realistic and attainable. Sometimes impatience stems from setting overly ambitious goals. Adjust your expectations to be in line with your capabilities and resources.

Instead of dwelling on the problem, shift your focus to finding solutions. Consider the setback and identify practical steps you can take to address it. Problem-solving promotes a sense of control and confidence.

Remind yourself of past challenges you've overcome and the skills you've developed along the way. This reinforces your ability to face adversity with resilience and patience.

Keep a determined attitude. Understand that setbacks are temporary roadblocks, not dead ends. Your patience in persisting through these challenges will strengthen your belief in your ability to overcome obstacles.

Embrace setbacks as opportunities for learning. Assess what went wrong and what you can do differently in the future. Every setback is a chance to become wiser and more prepared for future events.

Don't be afraid to seek support or advice from mentors, friends or family. Sharing your challenges and receiving guidance can provide emotional support and fresh perspectives.

Be kind to yourself during difficult times. Self-compassion helps you maintain a positive self-image, even when things don't go as planned. Avoid self-criticism and focus on self-improvement.

Keep a journal or a record of your journey in surviving setbacks with grace. Note how you approached challenges, your reactions and the outcomes. Over time, you'll notice your growing patience and resilience.

CHAPTER 7: EMPATHY

The bond between a dog and its human goes beyond mere attachment; it's a profound connection rooted in empathy, trust and unconditional love. Dogs, as social and pack-oriented beings, have empathy woven into their very nature. Dogs have an incredible ability to tune in to our emotions with amazing precision. Whether it's joy, sadness, fear or anxiety, they seem to sense it all. These emotional detectives quickly pick up on subtle cues in our body language and changes in our tone of voice. On our difficult days, they respond with comforting gestures, snuggling close or tenderly nuzzling our hands. And when happiness fills the air, they join the celebration with tails wagging and an infectious joy that mirrors our own. This empathetic response can be a lifeline for some of us during times of grief, illness or stress. Some dogs are trained as therapy dogs, providing invaluable emotional support to individuals navigating challenging circumstances, which is evidence of their innate empathy.

A dog's empathy isn't limited to just humans but extends to other animals. They engage in communication and connection with other dogs, using body language and vocalisations to express their feelings and intentions. Whether it's through playful antics, comforting gestures, or their ability to sense when another dog is unwell or anxious, their empathy shines through in their interactions with other dogs. They don't just confine their empathetic reach to their own species; many form emotional bonds with animals from entirely different species. These cross-species friendships serve as proof of their incredible capacity to empathise with all kinds of animals. How can the empathy we observe in our canine companions encourage us to become better friends, partners and caregivers to those around us?

Have you ever thought about how empathy and emotional intelligence work together, shaping our capacity to connect with others and navigate the complex web of social interactions? It's like having a toolbox to help us understand and manage our emotions effectively. Within this toolbox, empathy is a useful tool. Empathy serves as the bridge that connects us to the shared humanity we all possess. It's about recognising that, just like us, every individual goes through a wide range of emotions, from the highs of joy to the lows of sadness, and they face unique challenges along life's journey. It means setting aside judgement and fixed beliefs, enabling us to truly listen and understand what others are experiencing.

Empathy forms the foundation of compassion and kindness, a powerful tool that allows us to build stronger, more nurturing relationships and develop a sense of harmony and belonging. It gives us the ability to step into someone else's shoes, helping us understand their perspectives and feelings. Adopting empathy opens doors to deeper, more meaningful connections with the people in our lives. By nurturing empathy, we not only feel heard but also genuinely understood and valued. When we extend our empathetic hand to another, we're essentially saying, 'I truly care about your well-being and emotions.' Trust and authenticity flourish within such relationships. People place their confidence in those who demonstrate empathy because they sense that their concerns and emotions are not only acknowledged but deeply respected. People yearn for their emotions and experiences to be acknowledged. Empathy fulfils this need, assuring them that their feelings are not only real but also profoundly meaningful.

Stepping into others' shoes can serve as an important technique for improving empathy and developing a deeper understanding. When you demonstrate your openness to understand someone else's point of view, you confirm the value you place on their emotions and experiences. This forms the base of healthy relationships and boosts your confidence in your ability to connect with others. In moments of conflict it enables a sensitive exploration of another person's feelings and motivations, often leading to positive conflict resolution. As you practice this skill you'll notice your empathy becoming sharper and more profound, boosting your self-confidence in social interactions.

When people sense that their emotions and concerns are understood and respected trust begins to grow. Trust forms the foundation of a bridge that leads to conflict resolution, and the more trust you cultivate, the more self-assured you become in navigating these bridges. Reflect on a relationship where trust played an important role in resolving conflicts. How did this trust influence your self-confidence when dealing with future disagreements within that relationship? Also, empathy sparks your creativity in problem-solving. When you understand one another's perspectives and needs, creative solutions can be found that serve everyone's interests. Have you ever taken part in a brainstorming session where empathy played a role in generating creative solutions? How did that experience enhance your confidence in addressing similar challenges?

This practice of adopting different perspectives offers an unexpected gift: it heightens your self-awareness. As you become skilled at understanding various viewpoints, you may start to identify your biases and assumptions. This increased self-awareness becomes your ally, guiding you towards personal growth and boosting your self-confidence as you learn to navigate your own perspectives and emotions more effectively. With each instance of adopting someone else's viewpoint, you're not merely building connections with others; you're also strengthening your bond with your own authenticity. Can you recall a moment when someone truly grasped your feelings and viewpoint? How did that experience make you feel, and how did it impact your confidence within that relationship?

Empathy can nurture emotional regulation, the art of managing and controlling your own emotions. As you develop this skill you become less reactive to life's challenges and calmer when facing adversity. Think about a situation where emotional regulation played a crucial role in your response. How might improved emotional regulation, nurtured through empathy, have impacted your self-confidence in handling that particular circumstance? This emotional resilience becomes a sign of self-confidence, allowing you to stand tall, confident in your ability to navigate the ebbs and flows of emotions gracefully.

Self-compassion and empathy complement the other. Now, let's consider self-empathy. Imagine it as gazing into the mirror of your emotions and honestly acknowledging the reflection you see. When we embrace our feelings without passing judgement, it's like wrapping ourselves in a warm, comforting embrace. Have you ever found yourself dismissing your own emotions as irrational? How might practicing self-empathy transform your approach to this? Beyond emotions, self-empathy involves tuning in to your own needs and desires. It's like attentively listening to your inner GPS, which directs you towards your true north. How do you believe a deeper understanding of your own needs could influence your decision-making and sense of purpose in life? Consider the role of self-empathy in managing stress and adversity. It's similar to becoming your own best friend during challenging times. Consider a time when you offered understanding and support to a friend in need. How did that experience deepen your appreciation for self-compassion and self-empathy?

Empathy serves as the foundation of compassion and kindness, enabling us to build stronger, more supportive relationships and giving us a sense of belonging. It improves our interpersonal skills, active listening and self-awareness, all of which play a major role in boosting our confidence in managing emotions and relationships. We've considered the role of empathy in resolving conflicts, transforming tense moments into opportunities for understanding. Lastly, we've explored the impact of self-empathy and the interaction between self-compassion and empathy, increasing our emotional intelligence and self-confidence. Empathy paves the way for a more compassionate and self-assured way of life, both in our self-relationship and in our interactions with others. Give the following exercises a try. They are designed not only to reinforce the lessons in this chapter but to empower you to put them into practice in your daily life.

◆ ◆ ◆

Exercise 1: Active Listening

The aim of this exercise is to develop your active listening skills, a fundamental part of empathy. By consistently practicing active listening, you can strengthen your empathy and develop more meaningful connections with the people in your life. This exercise helps you become a better listener, allowing you to genuinely understand and support others in their experiences and emotions.

Instructions

Choose a friend or family member with whom you'd like to practice active listening. Ask if they are willing to participate in this exercise with you.

Find a quiet and comfortable place where you and your partner can sit down without distractions. Turn off or silence any electronic devices that may disrupt your focus.

Briefly explain the purpose of the exercise to your partner. Let them know that you want to practice active listening to better understand their perspective and feelings. Ensure they understand that you are committed to giving them your full attention.

Your partner will begin the conversation by sharing their thoughts, feelings or a specific topic of their choice. Encourage them to speak openly and honestly, and let them lead the discussion.

While your partner speaks, maintain eye contact to show that you are engaged and attentive.

Keep your posture open and receptive, avoiding any defensive or closed-off gestures.

Use non-verbal cues like nodding and smiling to show that you are actively listening and empathising.

Resist the impulse to interrupt with your thoughts, opinions or advice. Your goal is to focus only on your partner's words and emotions.

After your partner has finished speaking or has taken a pause, reflect back on what they've shared. You can do this by paraphrasing or summarising their main points. For example, you might say, 'So, if I understand correctly, you're feeling [emotion] because [reason]?'

To deepen your understanding, ask open-ended questions that encourage your partner to share more. For instance, you can ask, 'Can you tell me more about how that made you feel?' or 'What do you think might help in this situation?'

Express empathy and understanding by acknowledging your partner's emotions. Phrases like, 'I can imagine how that would be difficult,' or 'It sounds like you're going through a difficult time,' convey your empathy.

If your partner is comfortable with it, share your observations about their feelings and experiences. This can further demonstrate your empathy. For example, you might say, 'I noticed that when you talked about [topic], you seemed really passionate.'

If both you and your partner are willing, switch roles so that your partner can practice active listening as well. This allows both participants to experience the exercise from both sides.

After the conversation, take a moment to reflect on your experience. Consider how the exercise improved your listening skills and your ability to understand your partner's perspective.

Thank your partner for participating in the exercise with you. Express your appreciation for their willingness to share and connect on a deeper level.

Make active listening a regular practice in your interactions with others. The more you engage in active listening, the more natural and empathetic it will become in your relationships.

Exercise 2: Mirror Emotions

The aim of this exercise is to develop your ability to empathise with others by consciously mirroring their emotions. By doing so, you can create a stronger emotional connection, demonstrate your empathy, and provide support to those experiencing various emotions.

Instructions

Choose a social interaction with a friend, family member, colleague or acquaintance where you can practice mirroring emotions. It could be a conversation, a meeting or any situation where emotions are involved.

Before the interaction begins, set your intention to practice mirroring emotions. Remind yourself that you want to genuinely connect with the other person and show empathy for their feelings.

Pay close attention to the emotional cues of the person you're interacting with. Observe their facial expressions, body language, tone of voice and the words they use to express their emotions. Try to recognise their emotional state.

If the person appears happy, share in their joy. Smile genuinely and express your happiness for them. Use phrases like, 'I'm so glad to hear that,' or 'Your excitement is contagious!'

If they are enthusiastic about something, show enthusiasm as well. Share in their excitement by using enthusiastic language and gestures.

If the person is upset, acknowledge their feelings without judgement. Use empathetic phrases such as, 'I can see that you're really upset, and that's completely understandable,' or 'It sounds like this situation is causing you a lot of distress.'

If they are sad or experiencing grief, express your condolences and offer your support. Say something like, 'I'm really sorry to hear that you're going through this difficult time. Please know that I'm here for you.'

As you mirror their emotions, also engage in active listening. Encourage them to share more about their feelings by asking open-ended questions, such as, 'Can you tell me more about what happened?' or 'How are you coping with this?'

While mirroring emotions, be genuine in your responses. Avoid overdoing it or pretending to feel something you don't. Authenticity is crucial for building trust and rapport.

If the person is going through a challenging time, offer comfort and support. Let them know that you're there to listen, help or provide assistance in any way you can.

Respect personal boundaries and avoid invading someone's space. Mirroring emotions should be done in a way that respects their comfort level.

After the interaction, take a moment to reflect on your practice of mirroring emotions. Consider how it affected the quality of your interaction and whether you were able to connect with the other person on a deeper emotional level.

Make mirroring emotions a regular practice in your interactions with others. With time and practice, it will become a natural part of your empathetic communication skills.

Exercise 3: Practice Non-Judgement

The aim of this exercise is to develop non-judgemental listening and communication skills. By suspending judgement and seeking to understand others' perspectives, you can enhance your empathy, build trust and foster more meaningful connections.

Instructions

Choose a social interaction with a friend, family member, colleague or acquaintance where you can practice non-judgemental communication. This can be a casual conversation or a more in-depth discussion.

Before the interaction begins, set your intention to practice non-judgement. Remind yourself that your goal is to genuinely understand the other person's perspective without forming premature judgements.

As the conversation unfolds, consciously suspend any assumptions or judgements you might have about the person or the topic being discussed. Be aware of your thoughts and reactions.

Practice active listening by giving your full attention to the speaker. Maintain eye contact, nod to show you're engaged and avoid interrupting. Let the person express themselves without feeling rushed.

Instead of making assumptions or offering quick judgements, ask open-ended questions that encourage the speaker to elaborate on their thoughts and feelings. Examples include:

'Can you tell me more about that?'

'What led you to that perspective?'

'How do you feel about this situation?'

'What has your experience been like?'

As the person shares their perspective, empathise with their emotions and validate their feelings. Use phrases like:

'I can understand why you might feel that way.'

'It sounds like this is important to you.'

'Your perspective is valuable.'

Be mindful of any prejudices or stereotypes that may arise during the conversation. Challenge these biases and remind yourself that each individual has unique experiences and viewpoints.

Sometimes, our natural inclination is to offer solutions or advice. In this exercise, focus on listening and understanding rather than trying to fix problems or provide immediate solutions, unless the person explicitly asks for your input.

Maintain a curious and open attitude throughout the conversation. Seek to learn from the other person's perspective, even if it differs from your own.

After the interaction, take a moment to reflect on your practice of non-judgement. Consider how well you were able to suspend judgement and whether it positively impacted the quality of your conversation.

Make non-judgemental listening a regular practice in your interactions with others. Over time, it will become a natural part of your communication style, fostering empathy and deeper connections.

CHAPTER 8: DETERMINATION

One characteristic of a dog's determination is the loyalty they show their humans. Come rain or shine, they stand firmly by our side, offering constant support and affection. It's a display of commitment that teaches a valuable lesson; the strength that comes from being unwavering in our determination to be there for ourselves and others, particularly during hard times. In their enthusiasm for play and exploration, they offer a valuable life lesson: the importance of introducing joy and wonder into our own lives. When we channel our determination towards activities that genuinely bring us happiness and fulfilment, we unlock the potential to strengthen our self-esteem and boost our overall confidence. Dogs often face hard times, whether it's health challenges or even traumatic experiences, but they show a determination to heal and press forward. In their resilience and unwavering spirit, they teach us a crucial lesson about the power of persistence. When life presents us with obstacles and setbacks, they can encourage us to face these challenges head-on, emerge stronger and build up our confidence in the process.

Dogs make amazing role models when it comes to unwavering focus. They zero in on a ball to catch or a scent to follow, tuning out all distractions. They are also champions of persistence; they don't give up, even when faced with challenges or obstacles. They keep trying until they succeed, teaching us the invaluable lesson of resilience. Also, dogs approach challenges and goals with unwavering optimism. They genuinely believe in their ability to succeed. Ever noticed how your mindset can impact your determination? Cultivating a similar optimistic outlook can bolster your confidence and encourage persistence in the face of adversity. Dogs are also flexible and open to trying different approaches when encountering obstacles. They adapt their strategy if one method doesn't work. How do you typically deal with challenges and setbacks? Embracing adaptability can be crucial in achieving your objectives. Lastly, dogs don't doubt their worth or capabilities, and they don't engage in self-criticism. This unwavering self-approval can be a powerful source of determination. How do you usually talk to yourself when facing challenges? Practicing self-approval, just like dogs, can fuel your determination. By adopting these aspects of a dog's mindset – focus, resilience, living in the moment, optimism, adaptability, and self-approval – you can enhance your determination and, in turn, your self-confidence. So, how might you integrate these valuable lessons from dogs into your personal journey of determination and goal achievement?

There are some remarkable stories highlighting the unwavering determination of dogs. Hachiko, the loyal Akita dog, waiting for nearly a decade after his owner's passing, reveals the incredible power of commitment. Blind dogs navigating life with their other senses demonstrate adaptability and resilience, teaching us about overcoming challenges. The transformation of rescue dogs from fear to confidence highlights their remarkable determination and capacity for healing. Service dogs' rigorous training and unwavering dedication to assisting individuals with disabilities are nothing short of awe-inspiring. Search and rescue dogs' commitment to locating missing persons in perilous conditions underscores their unwavering determination. These stories serve as reminders of resilience and unwavering commitment, inspiring us to tap into our determination when facing difficulty, ultimately boosting self-confidence and personal growth.

Self-belief, also known as self-efficacy, is the ignition for determination. It's the faith in our abilities to overcome challenges and reach our goals. When we possess confidence in what we can achieve, it propels us to set ambitious objectives and dedicate ourselves to them; it's the foundation on which determination is built. Have you ever experienced that initial rush of motivation that comes from believing in yourself? Confidence serves as a wellspring of motivation, encouraging us to push forward, no matter the challenges we face. It acts as a protective barrier against discouragement and self-doubt. Have you observed how your confidence often keeps you going when the going gets tough? In moments of failure or setbacks, those with high self-confidence tend to be more resilient. They see setbacks as opportunities for learning and personal growth, rather than signs of failure. This resilience fuels determination, enabling us to bounce back with even greater resolve. How do you think your confidence has contributed to your ability to recover from setbacks and stay committed to your goals?

When we set our sights on ambitious goals and give it are all, something truly magical happens. Each victory, no matter how small, becomes another building block in are self-belief, like a confidence booster shot. Think about how empowered you feel when you achieve a hard-earned goal. Setting, pursuing, and reaching goals creates a track record of success, which forms the bedrock of self-assurance. Have you ever encountered a setback that ultimately led to personal growth and a stronger sense of self-confidence? It's this resilience in the face of adversity that defines determination. When you persist despite stumbling blocks, you're affirming to yourself that you have the capacity to handle whatever life throws your way.

As we steadily invest effort in our goals, we develop a positive self-perception as capable and persistent. Have you personally experienced this, where your commitment to a goal transformed how you see yourself in a more positive light? This newly formed self-image can become the foundation of self-confidence. We begin to view ourselves as someone who can overcome challenges and make things happen, which naturally builds self-assurance. The more you believe in your ability to achieve, the more likely you are to actually accomplish your goals. When we step out of our comfort zone we often stumble upon hidden reserves of inner strength we might not have known existed. Have you ever pushed beyond your comfort zone and discovered untapped reserves of confidence and strength?

The connection between confidence and determination sets in motion a potent feedback loop. When we establish challenging yet achievable goals and successfully achieve them, it boosts our faith in our abilities. This newfound confidence encourages us to set even more ambitious. Determination often involves making decisive decisions and taking calculated risks. Confidence is essential in effective decision-making. When we possess self-assurance, we tend to make well-informed choices and trust our judgement, even in uncertain situations. This, in turn, reinforces our commitment to the path we've chosen. Understanding this relationship between self-belief, confidence and determination can be a game-changer on our journey of self-improvement and personal growth.

We've discovered that determination, often fuelled by self-belief, serves as the driving force behind our ability to set goals, overcome obstacles, and continue through setbacks, continuously reinforcing our confidence in ourselves. Celebrating our achievements is similar to giving our determination a high five, contributing to our self-confidence, maintaining energy and confirming commitment to our goals. By applying these lessons from dogs, we have the potential to become masters of determination, ready to face life's challenges head-on and emerge stronger and more self-assured. Take a look at the following exercises and begin strengthening your determination skills.

Exercise 1: Overcoming Obstacles

The aim of this exercise is to help you identify obstacles or challenges that may strike as you work towards a specific goal. By consistently applying this exercise, you'll not only strengthen your determination but also become better equipped to handle challenges that may come up during your pursuit of any goal. It's a valuable skill that can lead to increased self-confidence and overall personal growth.

Instructions

Start by choosing a goal that you are currently working towards. It could be a personal, academic, career or fitness goal. Having a well-defined goal will make this exercise more focused and effective.

Take a sheet of paper or open a digital document. Write down a list of potential obstacles or challenges that you predict in your journey towards achieving your chosen goal. Be honest and thorough in identifying both external and internal obstacles. These could include time constraints, lack of resources, self-doubt or distractions.

Review your list of obstacles and rank them based on their potential impact on your goal. Consider which obstacles are most likely to occur and which ones might be the most challenging to overcome. Rank them from high to low priority.

For each obstacle, brainstorm possible solutions or strategies to overcome them. Be creative and open-minded during this step. Consider seeking advice from mentors, doing research or learning new skills as potential solutions.

Evaluate the resources, support systems or knowledge you may need to make your solutions more effective. This could include time-management tools, support from friends or colleagues or additional training.

Based on your list of obstacles and solutions, create a detailed action plan. Break down each solution into actionable steps with specific deadlines or milestones. Make your plan as clear and concise as possible.

Start applying your action plan, beginning with the most important and top obstacle on your list. As you come across challenges along the way, remain adaptable. Adjust your strategies if necessary and continue making progress towards your goal.

Regularly review your progress in overcoming obstacles and achieving your goal. Celebrate your successes, even the small ones, as this can boost your determination. Use a journal or digital tracker to record your journey.

Don't hesitate to seek support and feedback from mentors, friends or support groups. Sharing your challenges and successes with others can provide encouragement and new perspectives.

Remember that determination is a continuous effort. Stay committed to your goal, and keep using the strategies you've developed to overcome obstacles. Stay positive and remind yourself why you started this journey in the first place.

Exercise 2: Daily Routine for Determination

This exercise will help you establish a daily routine that incorporates dedicated time for self-improvement and goal-related activities. By following these step-by-step instructions, you'll establish a daily routine that not only helps to develop your determination but also brings you closer to achieving your goals. Over time, this consistency will become an effective tool for an increase in personal growth and self-confidence.

Instructions

Before you create your daily routine, it's important to have a clear understanding of your goals. Whether they are related to fitness, personal development, career or any other area, define them with clarity. Specific goals are easier to work towards.

If you have multiple goals, prioritise them based on their importance and urgency. Identify which goal(s) you want to focus on within your daily routine. This makes sure that you give them enough time and energy to make progress.

Take a look at your daily schedule and determine how much time you have available for your routine. Consider your work hours, family commitments and other responsibilities. Be realistic about the time you can dedicate to your goals.

Decide whether you prefer to incorporate your goal-related activities into your morning or evening routine. Some people find that starting the day with goal-oriented tasks sets a positive tone, while others prefer unwinding with these activities in the evening.

If you opt for a morning routine, set a consistent wake-up time that allows you to begin your day with focus. Ensure you get enough sleep to feel refreshed and energised.

Divide your available time into blocks or segments, each dedicated to a specific goal-related activity or self-improvement task. For example, you might allocate one hour for exercise, thirty minutes for reading and thirty minutes for skill development.

Use a planner, digital calendar or a simple to-do list to create your daily schedule. Assign each time block to its corresponding activity or task. Make sure you allocate time for breaks and meals as well.

Set SMART Goals: Within your daily routine, set SMART (Specific, Measurable, Achievable, Relevant, Time-bound) goals for each activity or task. SMART goals provide clarity and motivation.

Identify potential distractions that might interfere with your routine and take steps to minimise them. This could include turning off notifications on your devices or finding a quiet place to work.

If creating a new routine feels overwhelming, start small. Begin with a few goal-related activities and gradually expand your routine as you become more comfortable and consistent.

Keep a journal or use a habit-tracking app to monitor your progress. Record your achievements, setbacks and any adjustments you make to your routine. Tracking helps you stay accountable.

Regularly review your daily routine to assess its effectiveness. Are you making progress towards your goals? Are there activities that need more or less time? Adjust your routine as needed to improve your determination.

Determination often requires discipline. Even on days when motivation is low, commit to sticking to your routine. Over time, the consistency of your daily habits will help you build determination.

As you achieve milestones within your routine, take time to celebrate your successes. Recognising your progress can provide a significant boost to your determination.

Don't hesitate to seek support or an accountability partner who can help you stay on track with your daily routine. Sharing your goals with someone else can be motivating.

Exercise 3: Positive Self-Talk for Determination

The aim of this exercise is to develop the habit of practicing positive self-talk, which involves questioning negative thoughts and replacing them with affirmations that strengthen your determination and self-belief. By following these step-by-step instructions and consistently practicing positive self-talk, you can enhance your determination and build a more resilient and self-assured mindset. This exercise can be a valuable tool in your journey towards greater self-confidence and goal achievement.

Instructions

Begin by paying attention to negative thoughts that surface throughout your day. These thoughts might include self-doubt, criticism or thoughts that undermine your determination. Awareness is the first step to change.

To track your negative thoughts, consider keeping a thought journal. Whenever you notice a negative thought, jot it down. Note the circumstances or triggers that led to that thought.

Take each negative thought you've recorded and challenge its validity. Ask yourself questions like:

'Is this thought based on facts or assumptions?'

'What evidence supports or contradicts this thought?'

'Would I say this to a friend facing a similar situation?'

Challenging negative thoughts helps you see them more objectively. Once you've challenged a negative thought, replace it with a positive affirmation that reinforces your determination and self-belief. For example, if you had a thought like 'I'll never achieve this,' replace it with 'I am capable of overcoming challenges and achieving my goals.'

Compile a list of positive affirmations that resonate with you. These affirmations should address common negative thoughts or doubts you've identified in your thought journal. Customise your list to suit your specific needs. Examples include:

'I am determined and persistent in the face of hard times.'

'I believe in my ability to reach my goals.'

'Challenges only make me stronger.'

Incorporate the practice of affirmations into your daily routine. Set aside time, such as in the morning or before important tasks, to repeat these affirmations to yourself.

Combine positive affirmations with visualisation. When you repeat an affirmation, visualise yourself acting with determination and achieving your goals. This adds a vivid and motivating dimension to your self-talk.

Consistency is key to the effectiveness of positive self-talk. Even on days when you feel confident, continue practicing affirmations to reinforce your determination and self-belief.

When you encounter setbacks or challenges, be prepared to use positive self-talk to address any negative thoughts that may arise. Remind yourself of your affirmations and your determination to overcome obstacles.

Consider sharing your affirmations with a supportive friend or family member. They can offer encouragement and remind you to stay committed to positive self-talk.

Regularly review your thought journal to see if you're experiencing fewer negative thoughts or if you're effectively challenging and replacing them with affirmations. Tracking your progress can be motivating.

As you grow in determination and self-belief, adjust your list of affirmations accordingly. You may find that you're ready to tackle new challenges and address different areas of self-improvement.

After practicing positive self-talk for a while, reflect on how it has influenced your determination and overall mindset. You may notice increased confidence and resilience.

CHAPTER 9: GRATITUDE

You might be wondering, *Gratitude in dogs? How does that work?* Well, dogs have a remarkable ability to find joy in life's simple pleasures. They naturally appreciate every small act of love and kindness and teach us that gratitude isn't just about grand acts; it's about valuing the small everyday moments of happiness. Have you ever noticed how dogs can gain happiness and contentment from the most ordinary things? They have mastered the art of being thankful for life's little pleasures. Gratitude isn't only about saying thank you for what we have; it's about recognising the value of those things and how they contribute to our sense of self-worth. When we actively practice gratitude, our focus shifts from what's lacking in our lives to what's abundant and meaningful.

Begin your day with the simple yet powerful practice of appreciating life's little pleasures. Picture this: you soak in the gentle morning sun, relish a piping hot cup of coffee, and let the birds' songs outside your window fill your senses. How can these moments of gratitude influence your day and your sense of abundance? Gratitude is your gateway to not just acknowledging but celebrating your achievements, even the tiniest ones. Practice isn't just about thankfulness; it's a profound way to boost your self-worth, reinforcing your self-confidence. What's something simple you're grateful for today?

Gratitude has the power to redirect our focus away from what we might be lacking and shine a light on the abundance present in our lives. This shift in perspective is amazingly freeing because it helps us see our inherent worth, regardless of outer validations.

Just think about this for a moment. When you take a moment to appreciate your accomplishments, big or small, you're essentially declaring, 'I did this, and I'm proud of it.' It's much like our dogs, who don't need grand displays to feel loved and valued. You don't need massive achievements to recognise your own self-worth. When we practice the art of feeling grateful we are guided to find beauty in imperfections. In the same way that we love our dogs' funny little traits and oddities, so can we extend that same kindness to ourselves, accepting our unique qualities along with all our imperfections. When we genuinely appreciate who we are, warts and all, it becomes a profound act of self-acceptance. And guess what? Self-acceptance lays the foundation for self-worth and, in turn, self-confidence. So, what's one thing about yourself that you're truly grateful for, imperfections and all?

Have you ever taken a pause to reflect on your achievements, regardless of how big or small they may be, and genuinely felt thankful for them? It could be completing a challenging work project, passing a tough exam, or simply the satisfaction of checking off everything on your to-do list for the day. When you do this, you're essentially saying to yourself, 'I've got the skills and the determination to reach my goals.' It's like a little pep talk that not only boosts your self-worth but also fires up your self-confidence, getting you ready to tackle even bigger challenges.

Gratitude extends to your relationships too. Think about the people in your life who've been there through thick and thin, offering unwavering support and love. When you express gratitude for having them, you're recognising the positive impact you make in others' lives. It's a gentle reminder that you're genuinely valued and cherished, and that realisation can give a lift to your self-worth. Knowing that you genuinely matter to those around you can be a powerful catalyst for boosting your self-confidence. Who's someone special in your life that you're grateful for having by your side?

Gratitude can be your trusty sidekick when it comes to navigating life's twists and turns with a brighter outlook. When you face setbacks or challenges, approaching them with gratitude for the wisdom they offer can be really helpful as it shifts your view from thinking of them as failures to recognising them as opportunities for growth. Have you personally felt the connection between gratitude and self-confidence in your own life? This kind of resilience, fuelled by gratitude, strengthens your belief in your ability to conquer obstacles, having a positive impact on your self-confidence levels.

Gratitude isn't just about recognising the external blessings in our lives; it's also about appreciating the amazing person within us. When we nurture gratitude for who we are and the unique qualities that define us, it can work wonders on our self-image. Think of it as gazing into a mirror and not only appreciating your appearance but also the extraordinary attributes that make you, well, you. Dogs can teach us this valuable lesson. They don't engage in comparisons with other dogs; they're content with their own identities. Whether they're big or small, fluffy or sleek, they fully embrace their individuality. It's a lesson in self-acceptance that we can all learn from.

Now, let's relate this to our own lives. How often do we catch ourselves judging our appearance, our abilities, or our achievements, all while measuring them against others? This self-criticism can erode our self-image, leaving us feeling inadequate or unworthy. But what if we took a moment each day to express gratitude for our unique qualities? Perhaps it's your sunny smile that brightens up a room, your endless creativity, or your genuine kindness that leaves a lasting impact on people's hearts. These are qualities worth celebrating. When we practice gratitude for our individuality, it reshapes our self-image. Instead of fixating on perceived flaws, we begin to admire our strengths and positive attributes. We come to realise that, like everyone else, we are a work in progress, with opportunities for growth and self-discovery. What aspects of yourself are you most grateful for today, and how can we put this form of gratitude into practice? Well, it's as simple as creating a daily list of qualities, traits or achievements you're proud of. Maybe you're an exceptional listener, a cookery wizard, or a loyal friend. Jot them down and revisit the list regularly. This practice reinforces a positive self-image and bolsters your self-confidence.

Developing gratitude as a tool to enrich our self-image is an effective yet often underestimated path for personal growth and self-acceptance. Dogs teach us the lesson of embracing our uniqueness without the need for comparisons. By acknowledging and valuing the unique qualities that identify us, we can free ourselves from the grip of self-criticism and begin to be proud of our strengths and positive attributes. Gratitude's transformative power redirects our focus from our perceived failings to the inherent value we already possess, reducing the craving for external validation. While it's one thing to reflect on gratitude, it's another to express it, and there are a series of practical exercises at the end of this chapter that can help you develop gratitude and use it in your daily life. So, what's one thing about yourself that you're grateful for today? And how do you intend to weave these gratitude exercises into your daily life to enrich your self-image and bolster your confidence?

Exercise 1: Thank-You Notes

The aim of this exercise is to show gratitude by showing appreciation to people who have made a positive impact on your life. Writing heartfelt thank-you notes not only acknowledges their kindness but also reinforces your own sense of gratitude.

Instructions

Take some time to think about the people who have made a positive difference in your life. These could be friends, family members, colleagues, mentors or even strangers who have shown kindness. Think about specific actions or moments that had an impact on you.

Collect the necessary supplies for writing thank-you notes. You'll need stationery, note cards or plain paper, as well as pens or markers. Choose materials that vibrate with you and make the experience enjoyable.

Choose one or more people you'd like to express gratitude to. You can start with just one person or create a list of people you want to thank over time. Prioritise those who have had a recent positive influence on your life.

Begin your thank-you note with a warm greeting, addressing the receiver by name. In the body of the note, express your genuine gratitude. Be detailed about what they did or how they made you feel. Share how their kindness impacted you personally.

Make the note personal by sharing your thoughts, feelings and memories related to their kindness. Avoid general or overly formal language. The more personal and heartfelt, the better.

Don't be afraid to show your emotions in the note. It's okay to express how their actions made you feel and whether it brought you joy, comfort or inspiration.

Close the note with a sincere thank you. Use phrases like 'I'm deeply grateful for...' or 'Your kindness means the world to me.' Let them know that their actions were genuinely appreciated.

Sign the note with warmth and affection then seal the envelope and send it to the recipient. If it's someone you see regularly, you can hand-deliver the note for a personal touch.

Make writing thank-you notes a regular practice. Aim to send at least one note per week or month. As you continue this practice, you'll find that gratitude becomes part of your daily life.

Take a moment to reflect on how writing these notes made you feel. Notice the positive emotions that arise from expressing gratitude. This self-awareness can reinforce the practice and encourage you to continue.

Exercise 2: Gratitude Walk

The Gratitude Walk is a simple yet powerful exercise that can help you appreciate the beauty of the natural world and enhance your overall sense of well-being. Repeating this practice regularly can help develop a deeper connection with nature and promote mindfulness in your daily life.

Instructions

Select a time when you can take a leisurely walk without feeling rushed or distracted. Find a natural setting such as a park, forest, beach or any area with greenery and natural elements.

Before you begin your walk, take a few moments to prepare yourself mentally. Turn off your phone or put it on silent mode to minimise distractions.

Dress comfortably for the weather, ensuring you're warm or cool enough for the environment.

Begin your walk at a gentle pace. It's not a race; the goal is to be present and observant. As you walk, take a few deep breaths to centre yourself and clear your mind.

Pay close attention to your surroundings. Notice the colours, textures and shapes of the natural elements around you. Look at the trees, flowers, leaves, rocks, water or any other elements present.

Listen to the sounds of nature, such as birdsong, rustling leaves, or flowing water. While you observe nature, actively express gratitude for what you see and experience. You can do this silently in your mind or speak your thoughts aloud if you prefer.

Engage all your senses. Touch the leaves, smell the flowers and feel the ground beneath your feet. Taste the fresh air, if applicable, and fully immerse yourself in the sensory experience.

Stay in the present moment. If your mind starts to wander, gently bring your focus back to your surroundings.

Be non-judgemental and accept whatever you encounter without criticism.

Slow down your pace even further as you continue your walk. Take moments to sit or stand still and deeply contemplate the beauty and serenity of the natural world.

As you come to the end of your walk, take a few moments to reflect on the gratitude you've expressed. Think about how this practice made you feel and the positive impact it had on your well-being.

When you're ready to finish your walk, do so mindfully. Carry the sense of gratitude and connection with nature with you as you return to your daily life.

Exercise 3: Gratitude Jar

The Gratitude Jar exercise aims to develop a habit of recognising and appreciating the positive aspects of life by recognising moments of gratitude. It is a beautiful and clear way to remind yourself of the many blessings, big and small, that exist in your life. It encourages you to focus on the positive aspects of each day and fosters a mindset of gratitude, which can enhance your overall well-being and outlook on life.

Instructions

Select a jar or container of your choice. It can be a simple glass jar, a decorative box or anything that suits your style. Collect together small pieces of paper and a pen or pencil. Make sure they are easily accessible.

Select a visible and easily accessible spot in your home where you will place the gratitude jar. This can be your kitchen counter, bedside table or any place you frequent daily.

Whenever you experience a moment of gratitude, take a few moments to reflect on it.

Consider the people, experiences or things that have made you feel grateful. These moments can range from simple daily pleasures like a warm cup of tea, a kind gesture from a friend, a beautiful sunset or a personal achievement.

On a small piece of paper write down what you are grateful for. Be specific and heartfelt in your descriptions. For example, 'I'm grateful for my partner's support during a challenging time,' or 'I'm thankful for the laughter shared with friends during our meal.'

Fold the piece of paper and place it gently into the Gratitude Jar.

There's no need to date the notes, but you can if you prefer to track the timing of your moments of gratitude.

Aim to jot down moments of gratitude regularly. You can do this daily, weekly or whenever you feel inspired. The key is consistency; the more you practice, the more you'll notice and appreciate the positive aspects of your life.

Set aside times to review the notes in the jar. You can do this weekly, monthly or whenever you feel the need. As you read each note, take a moment to relive the feelings of gratitude associated with it.

Reflect on how your perspective on life may have shifted since you started this practice. Notice any changes in your mindset, mood or overall sense of well-being.

You can choose to keep your Gratitude Jar practice private, or you can share it with loved ones. Sharing your moments of gratitude can inspire others to adopt a similar practice.

This practice is not meant to have an endpoint. Continue to add moments of gratitude to your jar, even as you review and appreciate the ones you've collected. Over time, your gratitude jar will become a beautiful illustration of the positivity and gratitude in your life.

CHAPTER 10: FORGIVENESS

Dogs offer us helpful lessons in forgiveness. They have an ability to release past grievances and move forward, free from grudges or resentment. Think about a rescued dog, one that has endured neglect or abandonment. Over time, in a loving and secure environment, these dogs begin to rebuild their trust in humans. It's as if they hit a reset button on their hearts, choosing to give humanity another chance. They forgive, not just once but sometimes repeatedly, demonstrating an incredible capacity for love and trust. Dogs inspire us to tap into the incredible power of forgiveness, freeing ourselves from the chains of resentment and embracing a more compassionate world. Why are dogs so quick to forgive, and what valuable insights can we humans gain from their extraordinary ability to leave the past behind? How might embracing forgiveness become an important step in our journey towards emotional healing, ultimately leading to greater self-assurance and inner strength?

Dogs live entirely in the present; they don't hold on to past grievances or fret about the future. They possess the remarkable ability to forgive, forget and wholeheartedly embrace each new day as a fresh adventure. In doing so, they open the door to more joy and fulfilment in their lives. It's as though they're sending us a message: 'Why waste precious time carrying grudges when there's a world full of life to experience and love to share?' When we hold on to resentment, it's like carrying around a heavy backpack loaded with bricks. And what does this weight do? It burdens us, both physically and emotionally. What if we could release the grip of the past, stop dwelling on our mistakes, and fully engage ourselves in the present moment? We'd free ourselves from the burdens of grudges and guilt, ready to embrace each moment with an open heart. Embracing this dog-like approach to forgiveness has the potential to lead us to a life that's considerably lighter and more fulfilling.

How can we shed that emotional baggage and fully embrace the present? What does this process involve? Firstly, it's essential to understand that letting go doesn't mean we ignore what happened or minimise the pain we endured. It's not about excusing the actions of those who hurt us. Instead, it's about facing what occurred, understanding its impact on us, and then making a deliberate choice to release the bitterness, resentment and anger. To truly forgive, we can learn from dogs who do this instinctively. We must acknowledge our emotions, gain insight into them and then make the decision to let them go. It's about freeing ourselves from the past and fully immersing ourselves in the present. When we achieve this, we not only lighten a burden but also open ourselves up to the possibility for increased happiness and inner peace. It's a personal, transformative journey, promising a brighter, lighter future.

Dogs shower us with love, wholeheartedly accepting us, flaws and all. They don't cling to our past mistakes or expect us to be perfect. In their eyes, we are always more than enough, just as we are. So, can we take a page from their book and offer ourselves the same kindness and self-acceptance? Imagine your dog, tail wagging with pure joy as you walk through the door, thrilled to see you, regardless of any mistakes you may have had that day. It's a powerful image, encouraging us to practice that same unwavering love and self-acceptance towards ourselves. In doing so, we create room for personal growth and cast off the heavy weight of self-blame, adopting instead a mindset of self-compassion.

Forgiveness and empathy often go hand in hand, and dogs are exceptional guides in demonstrating this powerful connection.

They excel in empathy, effortlessly understanding another's perspective, emotions and experiences, responding with unwavering love. Unlike getting caught up in the right or wrong of a situation, they simply accept and offer love. Now, picture applying this approach to your human relationships. In moments of disagreement or conflict, what if, instead of stubbornly clinging to your viewpoint, you took a step back and genuinely tried to grasp the other person's perspective? This act of empathy can bridge gaps and resolve tension. It's like stepping into their shoes and seeing the world from their point of view. Empathy doesn't require you to agree with them, but it does soften your stance, making forgiveness and connection possible. Choosing to build bridges instead of walls isn't just about coexisting; it's a path to deeper, more meaningful relationships. When you construct walls, you isolate yourself and shut others out. However, when you build bridges, you create pathways for connection, understanding and love. It's a powerful message: 'I see you, I hear you, and I value our relationship more than being right.'

Picture this scenario: You've endured one of those patience-testing days where the universe seems determined to throw every possible problem your way. Tired and irritable, you finally arrive home, only to step on your dog's tail, a painful experience for both of you. Now, if it were a human in the same situation, you might expect cries of pain, some choice words, and lingering resentment, but despite the pain, your loyal dog gazes up at you with forgiving eyes, wags their tail, and seems to convey, 'It's all right, I still love you.' Their hearts are ready to forgive, regardless of what happens. They have a natural ability to let go and offer forgiveness, and it's a quality that offers lessons about releasing grudges, nurturing emotional healing and boosting our self-confidence.

Forgiveness, in a way, resembles decluttering your emotional closet. Imagine this: you have this dusty box stashed away in a corner, labelled 'past grudges and resentment,' and it's been there for ages. Each time you dwell on what someone did to you or how they wronged you, you're tossing more items into that box. It's like adding extra weight to an already heavy backpack you're carrying through life. This baggage affects your mood, your perspective and your self-confidence. But here's where the magic unfolds: forgiveness. It's challenging to feel truly confident when the past keeps weighing you down, isn't it? When you decide to forgive, it's like opening that box and, one item at a time, discarding the things that have been dragging you down. It's not about excusing what happened; it's about declaring, 'I deserve to be free from this burden.' You're not just releasing the other person; you're liberating yourself from the chains of the past. It's like shedding that heavy backpack and standing a bit taller. And as you stand taller, your self-confidence naturally receives a boost.

Dogs offer us invaluable lessons in forgiveness, which impacts on our emotional healing and self-confidence. Their ability to let go of past grievances and approach each day with an open heart is inspiring. Whether it's a rescue dog rebuilding trust or their natural ability to release baggage and embrace the present, dogs teach us about the power of forgiveness. To follow their lead, we need to acknowledge our emotions, understand the importance of letting go and embrace a journey towards a brighter and lighter future. Forgiveness isn't about condoning actions but about freeing ourselves from the weight of the past. It's a personal and transformative journey that can lead to greater emotional well-being and self-assuredness. So, let's embrace forgiveness, just as dogs do, and open ourselves to a life full of love, compassion and self-acceptance. To value the lesson of forgiveness we receive from dogs, I encourage you to embrace the following exercises to develop forgiveness in your life.

Exercise 1: Self-forgiveness

The aim of this exercise is to help you develop self-forgiveness as an essential foundation for forgiving others. By taking the time to forgive yourself first, you create a foundation of self-compassion that can make forgiving others a more natural and empathetic process. This exercise is an essential step towards emotional healing and greater self-assurance.

Instructions

Find a quiet and comfortable place where you won't be disturbed. This exercise requires self-reflection, so choose a time when you can focus without distractions.

Begin by acknowledging the mistakes or shortcomings that have been weighing on your mind. These could be recent incidents or events from your past.

Reflect on the emotions associated with these mistakes. Are you feeling guilt, shame or regret? Recognise and accept these feelings without judgement.

Imagine you're talking to a close friend who has made a similar mistake. What would you say to comfort and support them? Extend the same kindness and understanding to yourself. Remind yourself that everyone makes mistakes; it's a part of being human.

In a journal or on a piece of paper, write a letter of self-forgiveness. Address it to yourself as if you were writing to a friend. Be honest about your feelings and actions, and express your forgiveness. Use phrases like, 'I forgive myself for...' and 'I release myself from the weight of...'

After writing the letter, take a deep breath, and visualise yourself releasing the weight of self-blame and guilt. Imagine it lifting from your shoulders and dissolving into the air.

Create positive affirmations related to self-forgiveness. For example, 'I am worthy of forgiveness,' 'I accept myself with all my imperfections' or 'I release the past and embrace self-forgiveness.'

Self-forgiveness may not happen instantly. It's a process that might require several repetitions of this exercise. Be patient with yourself, and revisit it whenever you feel the need.

Regularly reflect on how practicing self-forgiveness has affected your self-esteem, self-confidence and overall well-being. Notice any positive changes in your attitude and relationships.

Once you've made progress in forgiving yourself, you'll likely find it easier to extend forgiveness to others. Remember that forgiving others doesn't mean condoning their actions; it's about freeing yourself from resentment and fostering emotional healing.

Exercise 2: Empathy Exercises

The aim of this exercise is to cultivate empathy, which is a crucial skill for forgiveness. By understanding the other person's perspective and motivations, you can foster forgiveness and build more meaningful relationships.

Instructions

Choose a situation or conflict in your life for which you are seeking forgiveness. This could involve a friend, family member, colleague or anyone with whom you have a strained relationship.

Take a moment to reflect on the situation from the other person's point of view. Try to understand their emotions, thoughts and motivations. Consider factors such as their background, experiences and current circumstances.

If possible, have a conversation with the other person to gain insight into their viewpoint. Ask open-ended questions that encourage them to share their feelings and thoughts. For example, you might ask, 'How did you feel when this happened?' or 'What were your intentions at that time?'

When the other person shares their perspective, practice active listening. Pay close attention to their words, tone and body language. Avoid interrupting or immediately offering your own point of view.

Put aside any judgements or fixed notions you may have about the situation. Your goal is to truly understand their perspective without making assumptions.

Try to empathise with the emotions they experienced during the situation. Were they angry, hurt, frustrated or confused? Put yourself in their shoes and imagine how you would feel in a similar situation.

Take into account their life experiences, values and beliefs. These factors can significantly influence their actions and reactions in the given situation.

After gaining a deeper understanding of their perspective, write a reflection in your journal or on a piece of paper. Describe what you've learned about their viewpoint and how it has influenced your view of the situation.

Look for areas of common ground or shared experiences that you and the other person may have. This can help build a bridge towards forgiveness and reconciliation.

Remind yourself that the other person is human, just like you, and is capable of making mistakes. Embrace the idea that understanding their perspective can lead to forgiveness and healing.

Empathy is a skill that can be developed and strengthened over time. Make an effort to practice empathy in various aspects of your life, not just in situations requiring forgiveness. This can enhance your relationships and overall emotional well-being.

Exercise 3: Visualisation

The aim of this exercise is to use the power of visualisation to make the process of forgiveness more visible and emotionally freeing. By mentally releasing the burden of a grudge or resentment, you can promote forgiveness and emotional healing.

Instructions

Choose a quiet and comfortable space where you won't be interrupted. Sit or lie down in a relaxed position.

Close your eyes to reduce outside distractions and focus your attention inward.

Begin with a few deep breaths to relax your body and calm your mind. Inhale deeply through your nose, hold for a moment, and then exhale slowly through your mouth.

Select a specific grudge or burden that you want to forgive. It could be related to a person, an event or a situation that has been weighing on your mind.

With your eyes closed, imagine the burden as a physical object or weight. Visualise it clearly in your mind, picturing its size, shape and colour. Recognise that this burden represents the grudge or resentment you've been holding on to.

In your visualisation, see yourself holding onto this burden. Feel the weight of it on your shoulders or in your hands. As you continue to breathe deeply, imagine making a conscious choice to release it.

Visualise the burden slowly lifting away from you. Sense the relief and lightness that comes with letting go. Picture it floating away or disappearing into the distance.

As you release the burden, say to yourself, either silently or aloud, 'I forgive (the person or situation).' Repeat this affirmation several times, emphasising your willingness to forgive and move forward.

Now, imagine yourself standing or sitting without the weight of the burden. Visualise a sense of freedom and emotional release. Feel the relief and peace that forgiveness brings.

Allow yourself to experience positive emotions associated with forgiveness, such as compassion, empathy and understanding. Visualise these emotions filling the space previously occupied by the burden.

Slowly open your eyes, and take a moment to reflect on the visualisation experience. Notice how you feel after letting go of the grudge or burden in your mind.

Consider keeping a journal to record your thoughts and feelings about the visualisation exercise. Write down any insights, emotions or changes in perspective that arose during the process.

Forgiveness may require repeated efforts, especially for deep-seated grudges or resentments. You can repeat this visualisation exercise as often as necessary to reinforce the process of forgiveness and emotional healing.

CHAPTER 11: COMMUNICATION

Dogs use a combination of sounds and body language to reveal their feelings and demonstrate intentions. From the enthusiastic welcome home bark to the alert intruder alert bark, their distinct barks indicate different situations. It's not just sounds that they use to communicate; dogs are masters of body language. They use their whole body to communicate. A tail wag is a clear sign of joy, a relaxed posture implies contentment, and a tucked tail with lowered ears reveals fear or submission. Dogs display their emotional world on their bodies, allowing us to understand what they're feeling and what they intend. Even the smallest actions, like placing a paw on your leg, communicate their desire for attention and affection. Dogs are unapologetic in expressing their hunger, playfulness, or the need to go outside, demonstrating clarity and confidence in their communication. So, how can we take inspiration from dogs to improve our own communication skills and authenticity?

The saying, 'Eyes are the windows to the soul,' is so true when it comes to the world of communicating with dogs. Think about those moments when you've had a heartfelt 'conversation' with a dog just by looking into their eyes. It's as if their eyes can reveal their very soul. Their gaze can communicate deep trust and love, or they might show fear and unease. Now, imagine what it would be like if we were equally open and honest, sharing our emotions through body language as dogs do. This is where the valuable lessons of authenticity and emotional transparency comes into play, potentially transforming the way we connect and communicate with each other.

Communication can be a complicated puzzle for humans, unlike dogs who keep it refreshingly straightforward. We humans tend to hide behind the veils of diplomacy, social norms and the fear of judgement, often resulting in our true feelings being concealed and misunderstood. But imagine the liberating feeling of shedding this burden and expressing our emotions without fear. Inspired by dogs, open communication doesn't mean recklessly venting our feelings or disregarding the emotions of others. It's about embracing self-awareness and emotional intelligence, understanding our feelings, why they exist, and finding the right way to communicate them with honesty and respect. So, how can we learn from dogs and bring more straightforward and open communication into our own lives? Have you ever experienced the benefits of being transparent with your feelings in your interactions with others?

Dogs show us that assertiveness can be a great tool for building self-confidence. They communicate with straightforward honesty, steering clear of passive-aggressiveness or ambiguity. With their straightforward and transparent communication, they offer a valuable lesson in the beauty of simplicity when expressing needs and emotions. They don't hold back, and they don't engage in mind games. In their world, there's no space for hidden agendas or mixed messages. When they're uncomfortable, they growl or bark, and when they're happy, their body language exudes joy. The lesson from dogs is clear: embracing clarity and honesty in our communication isn't impolite, but essential for self-assurance and for nurturing strong relationships. Dogs teach us that genuine expression not only gets our needs met but also builds deeper connections with others. Have you considered how embracing this dog-inspired approach enhances your self-confidence and your connections with those around you?

Think of moments when you needed to assert yourself at work or in a relationship. Did you express your needs and boundaries clearly, or did you hesitate, fearing the outcome? Dogs show us that assertiveness doesn't equate to aggression; it's about confidently advocating for ourselves and setting healthy boundaries. When we choose to use assertive communication, we express our thoughts effectively, reducing misunderstandings. This, in turn, bolsters our self-confidence, as we see ourselves as capable individuals who can navigate life's challenges with grace. Take a moment to reflect on the impact of open and respectful dialogue. Think back to those times when you could freely express your thoughts and feelings without the fear of rejection or dismissal. When you engage in open and respectful dialogue, ideas thrive, creativity increases and self-assuredness takes root. Imagine being part of a team or in a relationship where your ideas and opinions are valued and your contributions are met with respect and appreciation. You not only gain confidence in your abilities but also feel motivated to take risks and explore new possibilities. You are free from the constraints of self-doubt and the fear of ridicule.

Have you ever noticed the way a dog carries itself? There's an undeniable aura of self-assuredness, isn't there? Dogs have a lot to teach us about projecting confidence through their body language and mindset. Imagine a dog walking with a head held high and a purposeful stride. That's the embodiment of self-assured body language. Dogs don't slouch or shrink; they stand tall, radiating confidence. Their physical manner projects a powerful message: 'I know who I am and I have a purpose here.' Now, picture yourself in a similar scenario. When you enter a room or approach a situation, how do you present yourself? Are your shoulders squared, your head lifted, and your steps purposeful? Or do you tend to hunch, avoid eye contact or display nervous movements? Your body language sends an important message, not just to others but also to your own mind. When you consciously adopt confident body language, you send signals to your brain that reinforce your confidence. It's a mutual relationship: how you carry yourself influences how you feel, and how you feel impacts your body language.

Just as a dog's confident stride can inspire trust and respect, your self-assured posture can do the same for you. The power of confident body language goes beyond those initial moments but constantly reinforces how others perceive you in all your interactions. By maintaining eye contact, showing active listening, and using open and inviting gestures, you're sending out signals of engagement and assertiveness. Have you ever experienced the impact of body language on your confidence? Can you recall a specific moment when your posture and demeanour influenced your self-assurance and how others perceived you?

Confidence isn't solely about physical presence; it also hinges on your mindset. Dogs possess a beautifully straightforward mindset. They don't dwell on their shortcomings; they focus on their strengths. Celebrate your achievements, no matter how small, and let them boost your confidence. Next, practice mindfulness and immerse yourself in the present moment. Dogs don't fret over the future or dwell on the past; they enjoy the here and now. Mindfulness can ground you, ease anxiety and instil a positive outlook. Lastly, embrace a growth mindset. Dogs are continual learners, adaptors and explorers. They don't shy away from mistakes; they see them as opportunities to evolve. Likewise, view challenges and setbacks as stepping-stones to personal development. Instead of fearing failure, embrace it as a chance to become better. So, whether you're practicing your assertive communication or attempting to reinforce your confidence, remember that both body language and mindset are vital. Channel your inner dog: stand tall, appreciate the present and welcome every experience as a chance to grow. Embracing confident body language and nurturing a positive mindset can be true game-changers in your life. It's like unlocking your inner potential and letting your self-assuredness shine.

Dogs communicate with striking clarity, employing a range of sounds, body language and expressive eyes. Their genuine approach to expressing needs and emotions offers important lessons for us humans. We often complicate our communication with layers of diplomacy and social norms, hiding our true feelings. Dogs, on the other hand, teach us the beauty of simplicity and the transformative power of open and honest dialogue. They stress the importance of assertiveness, distinguishing it from aggression and presenting it as a means to ask for our needs to be met and to respect our boundaries. In addition, they show that projecting self-assuredness isn't solely about what we say but how we carry ourselves and the mindset we embrace. Their confident stride and straightforward mindset inspire us to stand tall, stay present and view challenges as opportunities for growth. By embracing these invaluable lessons, we can improve our communication skills and build deeper connections. I encourage you to take a look at the exercises that follow this chapter. These activities are designed to help you develop your communication skills, both verbal and non-verbal.

Exercise 1: Open Communication

The aim of this exercise is to practice open communication in your personal relationships, fostering honesty and trust. Remember that open communication is a skill that takes practice. Over time, it can lead to deeper connections and increased trust in your personal relationships.

Instructions

Choose someone in your personal life, such as a friend, family member or partner, with whom you feel comfortable practicing open communication. This person should be supportive and understanding.

Find a quiet and comfortable setting where you can have a private conversation without distractions.

Start the conversation by expressing your intention to practice open and honest communication. Let the person know that you value your relationship and want to strengthen it through openness.

Begin by sharing something that's been on your mind, whether it's a feeling, concern or something you'd like to discuss. Use 'I' statements to express your feelings and thoughts, such as 'I feel' or 'I think.'

After sharing, encourage the other person to express their thoughts and feelings on the topic or any other matter they wish to discuss. Create a safe space for them to be open and honest.

As they speak, practice active listening by giving your full attention. Avoid interrupting and allow them to finish before responding.

Respond to their thoughts and feelings in a non-judgemental and empathetic manner. Avoid criticism or defensiveness.

Reinforce the idea that open communication is about building trust and understanding. Emphasise that you both can express yourselves without fear of negative consequences.

Make open communication a regular practice in your relationship. Schedule time for these conversations and continue to encourage each other to share honestly.

After each open communication session, take a moment to reflect on what you've learned and how it has impacted your relationship. Adjust your approach as needed to improve communication.

Exercise 2: Eye Contact

The aim of this exercise is to practice and evaluate the impact of maintaining eye contact during conversations. Practicing maintaining eye contact can help you become more effective in your interpersonal communication. It can convey confidence, sincerity and active engagement in conversations, improving the quality of your connections with others.

Instructions

Find a willing conversation partner, whether it's a friend, family member or colleague. Ensure you have their consent to practice maintaining eye contact.

Pick a comfortable and quiet setting for your conversation. A distraction-free environment will help you focus on maintaining eye contact.

Start a conversation on a topic of mutual interest. It could be about your day, a shared hobby, or any other subject that allows for a natural discussion.

As you begin the conversation, make an effort to initiate and maintain eye contact with your conversation partner. Begin with brief moments of eye contact and gradually increase the duration as you become more comfortable.

Pay attention to your conversation partner's reactions. Notice if they also make an effort to maintain eye contact or if they respond differently to your increased eye contact. Their comfort level may vary, so be respectful of their response.

As you maintain eye contact, try to relax and maintain a natural breathing rhythm. Avoid staring intensely or blinking excessively, as this can be distracting.

While maintaining eye contact, focus on actively listening to what your conversation partner is saying. Engage in the conversation with genuine interest.

If you feel nervous or uncomfortable, remind yourself that maintaining eye contact is a skill that improves with practice. Take deep breaths to calm any anxiety.

Pay attention to your own feelings and thoughts as you maintain eye contact. Notice if it makes you feel more confident or if you experience any discomfort.

After the conversation, reflect on how maintaining eye contact affected the dynamics of the communication. Did it enhance the sense of connection? Did it convey sincerity and confidence? Were there any challenges or moments when you found it difficult to maintain eye contact?

Make an effort to practice maintaining eye contact in various conversations, both with familiar and new acquaintances. Over time, it will become more natural and comfortable.

Be mindful of cultural and personal differences when it comes to eye contact. Some individuals may be more or less comfortable with prolonged eye contact based on their background and experiences. Always respect their boundaries and adjust your approach accordingly.

Exercise 3: Body Language Awareness

The aim of this exercise is to raise awareness of your own body language and learn to adjust it to express confidence during interactions with other people. Becoming aware of and adjusting your body language can significantly enhance your ability to convey confidence and engagement in interpersonal interactions. It is a valuable skill that can positively influence how you are perceived and how effectively you communicate with others.

Instructions

Begin by observing your own body language in various situations. Pay attention to your posture, gestures and facial expressions. Take note of how you typically present yourself in different contexts, such as during conversations, meetings or social gatherings.

As you examine your body language, identify any regular patterns or habits. Are there individual gestures or postures you tend to adopt when you feel confident or less so? Make a note of any behaviours that may be undermining your ability to convey confidence and engagement.

Develop mindfulness by staying attuned to your body language in real time. Whenever you are in a conversation or interaction, make a conscious effort to notice your posture and gestures. Mindfulness will help you become more aware of how your body language aligns with your feelings and intentions.

Experiment with adopting confident postures and gestures. For example, stand or sit up straight, with your shoulders back and your chest slightly forward. Maintain an open posture by keeping your arms relaxed at your sides or gesturing with open palms. Avoid crossing your arms, which can suggest defensiveness.

Pay attention to your facial expressions, especially when listening or speaking. Maintain a warm and engaged facial expression by smiling genuinely (when appropriate) and maintaining eye contact. Avoid expressions that might be perceived as disinterest, such as frowning or looking distracted.

Observe confident individuals you admire and pay attention to their body language. Take note of how they carry themselves, their gestures, and how they maintain engagement during conversations. Try to emulate some of these behaviours.

Practice your adjusted body language in role-playing scenarios with a friend or trusted colleague. Have them provide feedback on how your body language comes across and whether it shows confidence and engagement.

If possible, record video of yourself in various interactions, such as during meetings or presentations. Review the recordings to assess your body language and identify areas for improvement.

Before important interactions or situations where you want to convey confidence, engage in positive visualisation. Picture yourself using confident body language and imagine the positive impact it will have on the interaction.

Make body language awareness and adjustment an ongoing practice. Continuously attempt to align your body language with your desired level of confidence and engagement.

Reflect on the impact of your adjusted body language in various interactions. Notice how it affects your own confidence and how others respond to you. Use this feedback to refine your body language further.

CHAPTER 12: AUTHENTICITY

Dogs embrace their true selves, flaws and all. Dogs don't perceive vulnerability as a sign of weakness; instead, they view it as an opportunity for connection and empathy. When they seek comfort or support, they don't conceal their vulnerability; they express it openly, inviting us to respond with care and affection. Let's imagine a familiar scenario: You've had a challenging day, and you return home, feeling drained and disheartened. Your dog's enthusiastic tail wag greets you, expressing their pure joy at your arrival. They don't hold back their excitement or worry about how they might appear to others. There's no concern about whether their enthusiasm is too much or if they should calm it. No, their sole focus is their sheer delight at seeing you, and they express it with their whole being. Have you ever experienced a moment when you felt truly authentic, without any need to conceal your feelings or true self? How did it make you feel, and how did others respond to your authenticity? What could you learn from your dog's unwavering authenticity and apply it to your own life?

Let's reflect on how frequently we, as humans, suppress our genuine emotions. We often refrain from showing our excitement, perhaps due to the fear of being perceived as overly enthusiastic or even childlike. Tears may be held back, our effort to appear strong and composed even when we're hurting. Society's expectations sometimes condition us to be reserved, conforming to a particular image that hides our true selves behind a mask of social acceptability. However, dogs serve as a reminder that authenticity is nothing short of a superpower. It's the remarkable ability to be real, to embrace vulnerability and to express our emotions without fear. When we witness a dog's unfiltered joy or their unwavering loyalty, it's undeniably touching. In their authenticity, they form deep connections with us, nurturing trust and love.

Authenticity doesn't equate to recklessness or inconsideration towards others. Instead, it's grounded in self-awareness and emotional intelligence. It's about acknowledging our feelings, understanding why we feel a certain way and discovering the appropriate way to convey those emotions with honesty and respect. Much like dogs openly communicate their needs, feelings and intentions without any pretence, we, too, can get value from being our genuine selves in our interactions with others. By living authentically, we find ourselves growing more confident because we're not continuously weighed down by the burden of pretending to be someone we're not. There's no need for constant self-doubt or worry about how we are perceived. Instead, we journey through life with a sense of ease and self-assuredness because we're rooted in our true selves. Have you ever experienced a moment when you felt the liberating freedom of being your authentic self in a conversation or interaction with others?

Embracing authenticity creates a powerful feedback loop that has a profound impact on our self-esteem. It allows us to gain a deeper understanding of our own identity and values, leading us to shift our focus away from seeking external validation and instead find our self-worth from within. This internal validation, deeply rooted in authenticity, lays the foundation for healthy self-esteem. Dogs teach us that authenticity isn't about seeking approval or conforming to others' expectations; it's about embracing who we truly are. When we accept our uniqueness, quirks and vulnerabilities, we become resilient in the face of criticism or rejection. The opinions of others no longer hold the same power over us because we have a profound understanding of our intrinsic value. When we're authentic, we naturally attract people who appreciate and respect us for our true selves, rather than for any facade we might put on. These connections, built on trust and mutual understanding, further elevate our self-esteem. We feel genuinely valued and accepted, reinforcing our belief in our own worth. What steps can you take to enhance your authenticity and the quality of your connections in your personal and professional life?

Embracing authenticity can be a challenging journey, particularly in a world that often exerts pressure to conform. It demands self-awareness, courage and the willingness to step out of your comfort zone. This process may even involve letting go of people or situations that no longer resonate with your authentic self. To begin your journey of embracing your authentic self, set aside time for self-reflection. Think about what truly holds meaning for you, what ignites your passion and what fills you with joy. Pay close attention to your thoughts and emotions, and don't be hesitant about expressing them authentically. It's important to remember that authenticity isn't about perfection or having everything perfectly figured out. It's about being genuine and embracing your individuality. Much like a dog that confidently wags its tail and barks with enthusiasm, you, too, can present your true self to the world. Recognise that your authenticity is your superpower, the key to unlocking greater self-esteem, and leading a more fulfilling life.

Have you ever held back from being your true self due to fear of judgement? What judgements do you fear the most? Are you apprehensive about falling short of social expectations, or perhaps you're worried about letting down someone close to you? It's important to pinpoint these fears as the initial step towards conquering them. Remember that you are not defined by the opinions of others. Just as dogs don't base their self-worth on what humans think of them, your worth isn't dictated by external judgements. Your intrinsic value is an unshakable foundation, and it simply comes from being your authentic self. To bolster this realisation, practice self-compassion and self-acceptance. Be as kind and understanding to yourself as you would be to a good friend. Understand that making mistakes and being vulnerable are part and parcel of being human. As you gradually peel away the layers of pretence, you'll discover that the fear of judgement starts losing its grip on you. Your self-esteem will take flight as you enjoy being unapologetically you. Keep in mind that it's a journey, and it's perfectly all right to take it one step at a time. Embrace your genuine self and let your authenticity shine, knowing that your uniqueness is an extraordinary gift to the world.

Dogs illustrate the power of authenticity, showing us the beauty of embracing our true selves. Their genuineness and vulnerability serve as invaluable lessons in connection and trust. We often hide our authentic selves behind masks to conform to societal expectations, but dogs remind us that authenticity is a superpower, an ability to be real, to express emotions openly and honestly. By adopting this trait, we free ourselves from the shackles of pretence and external validation, nurturing a deeper understanding of our identity and values. This internal validation, grounded in authenticity, strengthens our self-esteem, making us more resilient in the face of judgement or rejection. We attract genuine connections and acceptance, reinforcing our belief in our intrinsic worth. Embracing authenticity isn't about perfection; it's about unveiling our unique, genuine selves to the world. Although it may require courage and self-reflection, remember that authenticity is your superpower, unlocking greater self-esteem and a more fulfilling life. By peeling away the layers of preteens, you can find your authentic self and experience the extraordinary gift of embracing your true uniqueness. Why not give the following exercises a try? They'll help you understanding the ideas in this chapter and encourage you to put them into practice in your everyday life. Remember that embracing authenticity is a journey, and it's okay to take small steps towards becoming more genuine in your interactions and self-expression. Each of these exercises can help you develop a deeper understanding of your authentic self and boost your self-esteem along the way.

Exercise 1: Authentic Self-Reflection

The aim of this exercise is to assist with exploring your authentic self, including your values, passions and sources of genuine happiness. By doing so, you can gain a deeper understanding of your true identity and enhance your self-esteem.

Instructions

Choose a quiet and comfortable space where you won't be disturbed during your self-reflection. This could be a cozy corner in your home, a park, or any place where you can relax and focus.

Have a notebook or journal and a pen or pencil ready. These tools will help you document your thoughts and insights.

Take a few moments to practice mindfulness or deep breathing to centre yourself and clear your mind. This will help you approach the exercise with a calm and open mindset.

Start by thinking about your core values. What principles or beliefs are most important to you in life? Consider values like honesty, compassion, creativity, integrity, family, friendship or any others that resonate with you. Write down a list of these values.

Next, think about the activities, hobbies or interests that ignite your passion and enthusiasm. Think about what you love to do in your free time or what makes you lose track of time when you're engaged in it. Make a list of your passions, whether they are related to your work, hobbies or personal interests.

Reflect on the experiences, moments or circumstances that bring you genuine happiness. These could be simple joys, such as spending time with loved ones, taking a long walk in nature, reading a good book, or achieving a personal goal. Write down the things that consistently make you happy.

Recollect instances in your life when you felt most authentic and true to yourself. These could be moments when you expressed your opinions, pursued your interests without hesitation, or simply felt at ease being who you are. Reflect on what made those moments special and why you felt so authentic.

Take some time to review what you've written. Look for common themes, connections, or overlaps between your values, passions and sources of happiness. Consider how these aspects align with your current life and whether there are areas where you can integrate them more fully.

Based on your self-reflection, consider setting intentions or goals for how you can bring more of your authentic self into your daily life. This might involve making small changes in your routines, seeking out activities that align with your passions or nurturing relationships that support your values.

Conclude your self-reflection by expressing gratitude for the insights gained. Acknowledge the unique and authentic qualities that make you who you are. Embrace your authenticity as a source of strength and self-esteem.

Exercise 2: Identify Your Masks

This exercise helps to promote self-awareness by recognising the masks you adopt in various situations to conform to social expectations. By recognising these masks and understanding why you wear them, you can work towards embracing your authentic self and boost your self-esteem.

Instructions

Find a quiet and comfortable space where you can reflect and write without distractions.

Begin by thinking about the various roles or situations in your life where you might wear different masks. These roles could include your professional life, social circles, family dynamics or any other context where you adapt your behaviour.

For each role or situation you identified in step 2, make a list of the masks or personas you tend to adopt. These masks could represent certain behaviours, attitudes or traits that you believe are

Now, take each mask one by one and reflect on why you put it on in that particular situation. Consider the social or cultural expectations, perceived judgements or fears that drive you to wear these masks. Try to delve deeper into the underlying reasons for each mask.

As you reflect on the reasons behind each mask, think about how these masks might stray from your authentic self. Are there aspects of your true identity that you suppress or hide in these situations? Identify the values, passions and characteristics that may be overshadowed by these masks.

Consider how wearing these masks has affected you emotionally and mentally. Have you ever felt like you were compromising your authenticity or values? Reflect on any internal conflicts or stress that may have arisen due to these masks.

For each mask, weigh the benefits of following social expectations against the potential drawbacks of suppressing your authentic self. Consider whether wearing these masks has truly served your well-being or if it's time to consider a more authentic approach.

Based on your reflections, set intentions or goals for gradually shedding these masks and expressing your authentic self in these situations. Consider small steps you can take to align your behaviour more closely with your true identity.

Throughout this exercise, be kind and compassionate towards yourself. Recognise that wearing masks is a common human experience, and there's no need for self-criticism. Embrace the opportunity for growth and authenticity.

Make this exercise an ongoing practice. Regularly revisit your list of masks and your reflections to track your progress in embracing your authentic self. Celebrate your successes and acknowledge areas where you've made positive changes.

Exercise 3: Celebrate Imperfections

The aim of this exercise is to promote self-acceptance and boost self-esteem by shifting your perspective on perceived flaws and imperfections. By understanding how these qualities contribute to your unique story and the positive qualities they might reflect, you can embrace your authentic self more fully.

Instructions

Find a peaceful and comfortable space where you can reflect and write without interruptions. Have a notebook or journal and a pen or pencil ready.

Begin by making a list of the flaws or imperfections you often perceive in yourself. These could be physical attributes, personality traits, habits or anything else you tend to view negatively. Write down each perceived flaw without judgement.

Take one perceived flaw at a time and reflect on how it contributes to your unique story and identity. How does it make you unique? Think about how this imperfection sets you apart from others. Does it make you different or distinctive in some way?

Consider how this imperfection might be associated with positive traits or experiences. For example, a scar might be a symbol of resilience, or shyness might be connected to thoughtfulness and deep introspection.

For each imperfection, write a positive statement or affirmation that reframes it in a more positive light. For instance, if you perceive a scar as unsightly, reframe it as a symbol of your body's healing power and strength.

As you write these positive statements, take a moment to visualise how these positive qualities associated with your imperfections enhance your overall character and uniqueness.

Express gratitude for these imperfections, as they are part of what makes you beautifully human. Acknowledge that they are part of your personal journey and story.

Throughout this exercise, practice self-compassion by being kind and forgiving towards yourself. Recognise that nobody is perfect, and we all have imperfections that contribute to our individuality.

Make it a practice to revisit your list of perceived flaws and the positive statements you've written. Use this exercise as a tool for self-acceptance and boosting your self-esteem. Celebrate your imperfections as unique aspects of yourself.

If you feel comfortable, consider sharing this exercise with a trusted friend or loved one. Sharing your reflections and positive statements can reinforce the process of embracing your imperfections.

CHAPTER 13: COMPASSION

Can you recall a particularly difficult day at work when you trailed home feeling completely drained but your loyal dog was right there to welcome you at the door, their entire body wiggling with excitement? They might not understand the difficulties of your day, but they definitely sense your emotional state. In their unique way, they're communicating, 'I've missed you, and I'm here to make you feel better.' This compassion isn't confined to moments of sadness or when you're under the weather; it's a constant in your relationship with your dog. They're always ready to lend an ear, extend a paw or sit by your side as a silent yet steady confidant.

Dogs demonstrate a powerful lesson about compassion in action, reminding us that it's not just about words; it's about presence, support and creating a safe haven for self-expression. They don't pass judgement or dole out criticism; instead, they wholeheartedly offer love and understanding. The natural compassion of dogs is nothing short of remarkable, don't you think? It's as though they hold a hidden code in their hearts, a blueprint for acts of kindness and empathy. Compassion is a journey that commences with self-awareness and an acceptance of our shared humanity, acknowledging that, as humans, we all stumble and encounter challenges. When we embrace our own struggles with compassion, we cultivate a nurturing environment where growth and self-assurance can flourish. The beauty of this is that this compassion naturally extends to others, fostering deeper connections and understanding in our relationships.

This incredible knack that dogs possess teaches us something important about the combined effect of empathy and compassion. It shows us that we, too, can create deeper connections with others by tuning into their emotional well-being, by being a dependable support in times of need, and sharing moments of happiness and sadness. Dogs don't limit their compassion to just the human members of their family. They extend their kindness and empathy to other animals, and this innate ability to recognise and respond to the distress of others is proof of their compassionate souls. Have you ever experienced such a deep connection with others through empathy? Can you think of moments when you've been there for someone, offering support or celebrating their happiness? How can you follow a dog's lead and extend your compassion to a wider circle, just like their affection for other animals?

You might wonder if compassion and confidence have anything to do with each other. After all, confidence is often associated with traits like boldness, assertiveness and self-assuredness, while compassion seems to bring in a softer, more empathetic touch. Compassion is, in fact, a fundamental building block of self-confidence. When we approach both ourselves and others with compassion, we create an environment where growth, understanding and self-acceptance can flourish. This, in turn, provides a substantial boost to our confidence. Can you see compassion and self-confidence working hand in hand in your own life or in the lives of those around you?

Empathy, which is our ability to understand and share the feelings of others, serves as a bridge that connects compassion and confidence. Can you recall instances where empathy deepened your connection with others and, subsequently, boosted your confidence? When we exercise empathy, we're not only strengthening our relationships but also enriching our own emotional intelligence. This higher awareness of human emotions allows us to move through social situations with ease, and this, in turn, provides a considerable lift to our self-confidence, because when we can connect with others on a deeper, more empathetic level, we inevitably feel more capable and secure in our interactions.

Dogs have a remarkable way of accepting themselves as they are, unlike us humans who often contend with self-criticism and doubt. They don't dwell on past mistakes or worry about future mishaps; they simply live in the present, embracing every aspect of themselves with unconditional love. Have you ever observed a dog that may not fit the conventional standards of beauty, yet they strut with confidence and contentment? This is a powerful lesson in self-compassion. Dogs don't need external validation to feel good about themselves; they simply radiate self-assuredness by accepting their unique quirks and imperfections. So, how can we apply these lessons to our own lives? How can we embrace self-compassion and, in turn, boost our confidence and nurture a kinder, more confident self?

Picture this: You're walking down a familiar path, and suddenly, you trip and fall. What's your immediate reaction? For many of us, it's a stream of self-criticism and frustration. But what if you could react differently, as if you were extending warmth and understanding to a friend who stumbled? This is the essence of self-compassion, a practice inspired by the wisdom of dogs. It's like being that comforting friend to yourself, offering kindness when you need it most. Think about those moments when a friend comes to you, their eyes filled with tears, worried by a mistake they've made. Your immediate reaction is likely one of compassion, offering a comforting shoulder, a listening ear and soothing words of reassurance. You remind them that making mistakes is a part of being human, that it's okay to fall short at times, and that they're still a wonderful person despite their mistakes. It's second nature to be kind to a friend in need. Now, let's turn that kindness inward. How often do we offer ourselves the same warmth and understanding when we stumble or fall short of our own expectations?

This is where self-compassion steps in. It's about recognising your own humanity and understanding that, just like every other person on this planet, you are prone to make mistakes, face challenges and sometimes not meet your own high standards. And the most important part? It's not just okay; it's essential. In fact, self-compassion is the key to nurturing higher self-esteem. Now, how can you bring this concept into your own life? What are the practical steps to practice self-compassion and start being your own best friend?

We have read that dogs are masters of compassion. Their unwavering support and understanding creates an environment of growth and self-assurance, emphasising the connection between compassion and confidence. By extending compassion to ourselves we nurture a kinder, more confident self. Dogs teach us to live in the present, embracing our unique quirks and imperfections without the need for outer validation. Self-compassion, inspired by dogs, is about offering the same kindness and understanding to ourselves as we naturally provide to friends in times of need. Recognising our own humanity, embracing our mistakes and understanding that it's essential to fall short at times, are central to developing higher self-esteem. The journey of self-compassion begins with self-awareness and embracing our authentic selves, just as dogs do. Have you ever felt the transformative power of self-compassion and the boost it brings to your confidence? What steps will you take to incorporate self-compassion into your daily life, nurturing a kinder, more self-assured you? Are you ready to try the exercises that follow? They're a practical way to introduce and use the valuable lessons from this chapter in your life.

Exercise 1: Compassionate Self-Talk

The aim of this exercise is to practice self-compassion through positive self-talk. Self-compassion is about treating yourself with the same kindness and understanding that you would offer to a dear friend in times of struggle or self-doubt. By consistently practicing compassionate self-talk, you'll gradually shift your mindset towards greater self-compassion and self-acceptance, which are essential for building self-confidence and well-being.

Instructions

Begin by taking some time for self-reflection. Identify a specific situation or aspect of your life where you typically engage in self-criticism or self-doubt. It could be related to your appearance, abilities, past mistakes or any area where you tend to be hard on yourself.

Pay close attention to the negative self-talk that arises in this situation. What are the critical thoughts or beliefs you have about yourself? Write them down if it helps you to clarify your inner dialogue.

Challenge these negative thoughts. Ask yourself if they are based on facts or if they are false and outdated perceptions. Then, reframe these negative thoughts into kind, understanding, and encouraging phrases. For example, if you often criticise your appearance, replace it with something like, 'I am unique and beautiful in my own way.'

Take a notebook or journal and write down the compassionate phrases you've come up with. Make this list specific to the situation you identified in step 1. Create a list of positive affirmations or self-compassionate statements that counteract the self-criticism.

Commit to practicing compassionate self-talk regularly. This means consciously replacing negative self-talk with these compassionate phrases whenever you find yourself in the identified situation. It may take time to break the habit of self-criticism, so be patient with yourself.

Regularly revisit your journal and reflect on how your self-talk has evolved. Have you noticed a reduction in self-criticism? Are you feeling more self-compassionate and understanding? Celebrate your progress and adjust your compassionate self-talk as needed.

◆ ◆ ◆

Exercise 2: Act of Kindness

This exercise will help you to extend compassion to others through acts of kindness. Compassion isn't just about how we treat ourselves; it's also about how we interact with and positively impact the lives of others. This exercise encourages you to practice compassion by planning and carrying out a random act of kindness. By making compassion a regular part of your life through acts of kindness, you not only positively impact others but also enhance your own sense of well-being and self-assurance.

Instructions

Start by thinking about the type of act of kindness you'd like to perform. It could be something small or more significant, such as paying for someone's coffee, offering a sincere compliment, helping a neighbour with their shopping or volunteering your time at a local charity. The key is to choose an act that feels meaningful to you.

Decide whether you'd like to perform this act of kindness for someone you know, like a friend or family member, or for a complete stranger. Both options are equally valid, so choose what feels most comfortable to you at the moment.

Plan the details of your act of kindness. If, for example, you're planning to buy a stranger's coffee, decide when and where you'll do it. If you're complimenting someone, think about how you'll say your message sincerely. Preparation helps ensure that your act of kindness goes smoothly.

On the chosen day and time, carry out your act of kindness without expecting anything in return. Be genuine and kind in your approach. Your goal is to brighten someone else's day and contribute positively to their life.

After performing the act of kindness, take a moment to reflect on the experience. Consider how it made you feel to bring a smile to someone's face or to offer help. Reflect on the recipient's reaction and the impact it had on them. Sometimes, these acts create a ripple effect of kindness that extends beyond the initial recipient.

Write down your thoughts and feelings about the act of kindness in a journal. Describe the experience, how it affected you emotionally and any insights or learnings you gained from it. Documenting your acts of kindness can be a powerful way to track your personal growth and the positive effects of compassion.

Widen the practice of compassion through acts of kindness beyond this exercise. Make it a habit to look for opportunities to be kind to others in your daily life. Small, consistent acts of kindness can lead to increased self-confidence and a deeper sense of connection with the world around you.

Exercise 3: Self-Compassion Letter

Self-compassion involves treating yourself with the same kindness and understanding you would offer to a special friend. This exercise encourages you to express self-compassion through a heartfelt letter written to yourself. This letter serves as a powerful tool for nurturing self-esteem, self-acceptance and emotional well-being. It's a reminder that you are deserving of love and compassion, especially from yourself, during both challenging and joyful moments in life.

Instructions

Choose a quiet and comfortable place where you can focus on your thoughts and emotions without distractions. It could be a cozy corner of your home, a park, or any location that allows you to feel at ease.

Have your writing materials ready. You can write your self-compassion letter by hand in a journal, type it on a computer or use any method that feels most comfortable to you.

Begin by setting the intention for your letter. Remind yourself that you are writing to offer comfort, encouragement and support to yourself, just as you would to a friend facing a difficult time.

Start the letter by addressing yourself with kindness. You might begin with 'Dear [Your Name],' or any greeting that feels appropriate to you.

In the body of the letter acknowledge the struggles, challenges or difficulties you are currently facing or have faced in the past. Be honest and gentle with yourself as you describe these experiences. This is an opportunity to validate your emotions.

Shift the tone of the letter to offer compassionate and understanding words to yourself. Imagine what you would say to a friend experiencing similar challenges. Encourage yourself with phrases like:

'It's okay to feel this way; I understand.'

'You are stronger and more resilient than you realise.'

'Mistakes and setbacks are part of life; they don't define your worth.'

'You deserve love, compassion and forgiveness, even from yourself.'

Take a moment to think about your positive qualities, strengths and achievements. Remind yourself of the aspects that make you unique and valuable. Encourage self-acceptance and self-appreciation.

End the letter with a warm closing, such as 'With kindness and compassion,' or any phrase that feels authentic to you. Sign your name.

After writing your self-compassion letter, keep it in a safe place. You can store it in a journal, save it on your computer or print it out. The goal is to have it readily available for moments when you need a boost of self-compassion.

Whenever you're feeling self-critical, overwhelmed or in need of self-compassion, revisit the letter. Read it aloud to yourself, allowing the words of kindness and understanding to soothe and comfort you. Remind yourself that you deserve the same compassion you readily offer to others.

CHAPTER 14: MINDFULNESS AND PRESENCE

Mindfulness, though often elusive in our busy lives, is second nature to dogs. They remind us that life is about embracing the present, finding joy in the little things and living each moment to the full. They lead by example, showing us how to enjoy the moment and be present. They're experts at shedding worries and immersing themselves in the now. When they're chasing a ball they're not just focused on the end goal; they appreciate the breeze, the texture beneath their paws and the joy that each moment brings. They're not worried by thoughts of the past or anxieties about the future. They urge us to slow down, breathe deeply and experience life in the here and now. Embracing the present moment can be a powerful tool in enhancing our self-confidence and overall well-being. What if we could let go of past regrets and future concerns and be wholly present in the here and now? Picture the simple pleasures in life, like the aroma of morning coffee, the tunes of your favourite songs or the touch of a gentle breeze on your skin, all without the constant buzz of thoughts and worries in the background.

Have you ever taken a moment to notice how your dog's company can take away your worries and stress? It's as if their mindfulness rubs off on you, pulling you into the here and now. Suddenly, your never-ending to-do list, work pressures and anxieties all fade into the background, leaving you with a refreshing sense of calm and crystal-clear thinking. What's great is how dogs have this unique way of making you feel like the centre of their universe. When they're with you, they're all in. Dogs have the ability to demonstrate the incredible power of living in the moment. Whether you're watching TV, tackling work or simply sharing a quiet moment, they're not preoccupied with the past or anxious about the future. They're 100 percent invested in the present, valuing your company like the most precious gift they could ever receive. What might the impact of being fully present in your daily interactions be for you and those around you?

Embracing mindfulness offers a great boost to our self-esteem. Picture it as a refreshing mental rinse that sweeps away self-doubt and silences the nagging voice of negative self-talk. When we're truly present in the moment, we release the grip of self-criticism and constant comparisons. We become aware of our inner thoughts and emotions and can swap judgement for self-compassion. Mindfulness trains your mind to focus on the here and now, unburdened by past mistakes or future worries. By observing your thoughts without judgement and replacing self-criticism with self-compassion, you pave the way for greater self-esteem. How could you benefit from shifting self-criticism to self-compassion in your self-esteem journey?

Have you ever been surprised at the way your dog listens to you? It's not a passive nod; it's a deeply engaged and wholehearted presence. When you chat to them about your day or share a silent moment, they're completely tuned in. This attentive listening is at the heart of mindfulness and can be a game-changer for relationships and self-esteem. Just think, when you genuinely listen to someone, you're acknowledging their feelings and experiences. You're telling them, 'I see you, I hear you, and your thoughts matter.' Now, imagine extending this mindful listening to yourself. When you listen to your inner dialogue without judgement, you're recognising your own emotions and experiences. You're treating yourself with the same respect and understanding you offer to others. This self-compassion is a powerful self-esteem booster. Beyond that, practicing mindful listening in your interactions can deepen connections and foster trust. When someone feels heard and understood, it builds appreciation and respect. This, in turn, positively affects your self-esteem, knowing you contribute positively to those around you. Embracing mindful listening to enrich relationships and nurture self-esteem is a simple yet powerful way to connect with others and, most importantly, with yourself.

The mindfulness lessons we learn from dogs encourage us to enjoy living in the present moment. This practice, often challenging in our fast-paced lives, is a gateway to enhancing self-confidence and overall well-being. Mindful living encourages us to slow down, let go of past regrets and future anxieties, and appreciate the beauty around us. These mindful dogs teach us to be present, to listen with our hearts and to connect deeply with others and ourselves. The journey towards greater self-esteem, self-compassion and self-assuredness is one of embracing mindfulness in everyday life. Remember that mindfulness is not a destination but a daily practice that gets you closer to your authentic self. To experience the benefits firsthand, carry out the following exercise regularly and observe how mindfulness and presence bring positive changes to your life.

Exercise 1: Mindful Eating

The aim of this exercise is to practice mindfulness and presence while eating. Mindful eating is not only about nourishing your body but also about nourishing your soul by being fully present with your food. This practice can lead to a deeper connection with your eating habits, improved digestion and a greater sense of satisfaction with your meals.

Instructions

Choose a meal or snack that you would like to eat mindfully. It could be breakfast, lunch, dinner or a simple snack like a piece of fruit or a handful of nuts. Choose something that you can comfortably eat without rushing.

Find a quiet and comfortable place to sit where you won't be disturbed. Ensure the environment is free from distractions like TV, smartphones or noisy background noise. You want to create a calm space for your meal.

Before taking the first bite, take a moment to really look at your food. Notice its colours, textures and how it looks on your plate. Notice any aromas that develop. Engaging your senses can help you become more present.

Take a couple of deep breaths to centre yourself. Inhale slowly through your nose and exhale through your mouth. This brief moment of mindfulness will help you transition into the eating experience.

As you take your first bite, do so slowly and intentionally. Pay close attention to the taste, texture and temperature of the food. Chew slowly, allowing yourself to fully experience each bite. Notice how the flavours evolve in your mouth.

While eating, engage all your senses. Listen to the sounds of your food as you chew, feel the sensation of the utensils in your hand and observe the way your food looks on the plate. This multisensory experience deepens your connection to the present moment.

As you swallow each bite, be aware of the process of swallowing.

Notice how the food moves from your mouth to your throat and eventually into your stomach. Take your time between bites, appreciating the experience.

Occasionally pause during your meal to reflect on your experience. How does it feel to eat mindfully? Are you noticing flavours and textures you might have missed before? Take note of any sensations or thoughts that arise without judgement.

Continue to eat mindfully until you've finished your meal. Be aware of any changes in your feelings of fullness and satisfaction. Eating slowly and intentionally often leads to a greater sense of satisfaction with smaller portions.

After completing your meal, take a moment to express gratitude for the food you've received. Reflect on the experience of mindful eating and how it can positively impact your relationship with food.

Consider incorporating mindful eating into your daily routine. As you practice regularly, you'll find that you naturally become more present during meals and make healthier food choices.

Exercise 2: Nature Walk

The aim of this exercise is to cultivate mindfulness and presence by enjoying yourself in the natural world. Nature walks offer an opportunity to reconnect with the world around you and find solace in the beauty of nature. By practicing mindfulness during these walks, you can reduce stress, improve your mental well-being and deepen your appreciation for the wonders of the natural world.

Instructions

Choose a natural setting for your walk such as a park, forest, beach or any place where you can be surrounded by nature. Make sure that it's a location that you find appealing and where you can walk leisurely without feeling rushed.

Wear comfortable clothing and the right footwear for your chosen environment. Dress in layers if needed, considering the weather and temperature.

Before you begin your walk, turn off or silence your phone and any electronic devices. This walk is an opportunity to disconnect from digital distractions and fully engage with the natural world.

As you begin your walk, take a moment to stand still and take a few deep breaths. Inhale through your nose and exhale through your mouth. Allow yourself to transition from your daily mindset to a state of mindfulness.

View your surroundings with an open gaze. Notice the colours, shapes and patterns in nature. Look at both near and far objects.

Listen to the sounds of nature. Pay attention to bird songs, rustling leaves, flowing water or any other natural sounds.

Take in the smells of the environment. Breathe deeply and notice any fragrances, whether they come from flowers, trees or the earth.

Feel the sensations in your body as you walk. Notice the ground beneath your feet, the temperature of the air and any textures you encounter.

As you walk, focus on each step you take. Feel your feet lifting off the ground, moving through the air and making contact with the earth again. Be aware of the subtle movements in your body as you walk.

Take the time to examine the details of nature around you. Notice the details of leaves, the play of light and shadow, or the ripples in a stream. Grow a sense of wonder as you explore.

Pause during your walk to reflect on your experience. Take in the beauty and serenity of nature. Acknowledge any thoughts or emotions that arise without judgement.

Try to connect on a deeper level with the natural world. Touch a tree trunk, feel the texture of a rock or sit quietly by a body of water. Allow yourself to merge with the environment.

As you come to the end of your nature walk, take a moment to express gratitude for the opportunity to connect with nature and for the beauty that surrounds you. Reflect on the sense of calm and presence you've developed.

Think about including nature walks into your daily or weekly routine. Regularly accessing the natural world can become a powerful mindfulness practice that enriches your life and increases your sense of presence.

Exercise 3: Body Awareness in Daily Activities

By practicing body awareness in daily activities, you can transform routine tasks into opportunities for mindfulness and presence. This exercise enhances your ability to stay anchored in the present moment and brings a sense of mindfulness to even the most ordinary aspects of your daily life.

Instructions

Choose a daily activity that you carry out without much thought. These could be activities such as washing dishes, taking a shower, brushing your teeth or making your bed. Choose one that you'll engage in mindfully.

Before you begin, set the intention to approach it mindfully. Remind yourself that this activity will serve as a mindfulness practice to enhance your presence in daily life.

If possible, eliminate distractions by choosing a quiet space where you won't be interrupted. Ensure that you have plenty of time to complete the activity without rushing.

As you begin the chosen activity, take a moment to pause and focus your attention on your breath. Inhale deeply through your nose, exhale slowly through your mouth and feel yourself becoming present.

Pay attention to the physical sensations of the activity. Feel the textures, temperatures and pressures involved.

Observe the details of what you're doing. Notice colours, shapes and any visual elements.

Listen to the sounds associated with the activity. Whether it's the flow of water, the swishing of a toothbrush or the clinking of dishes, be aware of the auditory experience.

Notice any smells associated with the activity. This may be the smell of soap, toothpaste or any aromas in your environment.

Maintain your focus on the task at hand. If your mind begins to wander or if you become distracted by thoughts, gently bring your attention back to the sensations and movements of the activity.

Pay close attention to the movements of your body as you perform the activity. Notice the muscles you engage, the range of motion and the coordination required.

As you complete the activity, take a moment to express gratitude for the opportunity to engage in this daily task mindfully. Recognise the richness and presence it brings to your life.

After finishing the activity, reflect on your experience. Consider how your view of the task changed when you approached it with mindfulness. Acknowledge any sense of presence or calm that emerged.

Include mindful engagement into more of your daily activities over time. The goal is to cultivate a habit of mindfulness in everyday life, allowing you to stay present and find joy in the ordinary.

Conclusion

Thank you for choosing this book to be part of your journey towards unshakable confidence. You have discovered how adopting the traits that dogs display, including presence, compassion, mindfulness and generosity, can serve as the perfect stepping-stones on the journey to building your self-confidence. You have experienced how these qualities can positively impact your self-esteem and overall well-being. As you move forward, hold these lessons close to your heart, while sharing the love and wisdom dogs show you with others, extending the cycle of positivity and gratitude in our world.

As with any journey, it's important to remember that building confidence is not a one-time event; it's a lifelong venture. You've gained insights and tools to support your progress, but the path ahead may have its share of challenges and setbacks. This journey is a practice, one that thrives on consistency, dedication and the willingness to learn from both successes and failures.

After each chapter, you've carried out exercises designed to put these principles into action. You've taken steps to live in the present, offer kindness and compassion, embrace mindfulness and share your generosity with the world. These practical exercises are the key to translating knowledge into wisdom and self-assurance. I encourage you to continue practicing these exercises regularly. Remember, it's in the doing that true growth occurs.

I hope you enjoy the journey ahead. Always keep an open heart and you'll find your confidence growing, your self-esteem blossoming and your inner strength soaring. The transformation may not happen overnight, but trust that every act of mindfulness, every expression of compassion, every exercise in self-compassion and every gesture of generosity will be a stepping-stone towards the confident self you will become.

Remember that the journey to mastering confidence is one that you are fully capable of. It starts with a willingness to embrace the wisdom shared in this book and to practice its principles. It's a journey that can lead to a more authentic, confident and self-assured you. Keep these lessons close to your heart, share them with others, and remember that, much like dogs, you have within you the potential to be your very best life coach. I wish you every success on this journey. Master your confidence, for you are more than capable, and the world is ready to see you shine.

As we come to the end of our journey into mastering confidence, I'm excited to let you know about the next book in our series. In *The Dog Life Coach's Guide to Weight Loss and Wellness*, we'll discover valuable lessons about weight loss, maintaining a healthy weight and overall well-being. In this upcoming book, you can look forward to discovering the dog wisdom that leads to a balanced and fulfilling life, embracing both physical and emotional health. Join us as we delve into practical strategies and exercises designed to help you achieve your health, weight loss and wellness goals.

Additional information

Thank you for choosing to read this book and I hope the knowledge you've gained has enhanced many aspects of your life. To continue your discovery to a more fulfilling and joyful life check out the following titles in The Dog Life Coach series:

The Dog Life Coach: Lessons in Love and Life

The Dog Life Coach's Guide to Weight Loss and Well-Being

If you have a keen interest in learning and want to explore how dogs can be your ultimate life coach take a look at our online courses here:

https://payhip.com/animalhealingtherapy

The Wisdom Within: Embracing Life's Lesson's Through Dogs

In this 8-module course you'll explore the remarkable qualities of dogs, such as loyalty, presence and intuition, applying their life lessons to enhance your well-being. Through practical exercises in intuition, mindfulness and animal communication, you'll develop emotional awareness, refine communication skills and achieve a newfound sense of balance, inner peace and fulfilment.

Take the next step and join us in the Dog Life Coach Club.

For exclusive updates, bonus content and the chance to connect with others on a similar journey we encourage you to sign up for our newsletter here:

https://subscribepage.io/TheClub

Joining the Dog Life Coach Club grants you access to regular insights, special offers, and a supportive community that shares a passion for dogs and the pursuit of a more fulfilling life. Here's to celebrating the lessons of loyalty, resilience, and love, and to living each day with the spirit of being more dog!

Enjoyed Mastering Confidence. Lessons from The Dog Life Coach? Here's what you can do next.

If you have a moment to spare I would really appreciate a short review. Your help in spreading the word is gratefully received.

BOOKS BY THIS AUTHOR

The Dog Life Coach. Lessons In Love And Life

I often struggle to believe in myself and my abilities. How can I develop more self-confidence and trust in my potential?

In today's hectic world I find it hard to live in the present and find joy in the here and now. I long for a sense of purpose and fulfilment. How can I discover my true passion and live a more purpose-driven life?

Trust is essential in relationships but past experiences have left me guarded. How can I cultivate trust in myself and others?

Transform self-doubt into self-acceptance, anxiety into empowerment and stress into serenity with The Dog Life Coach. Let a dog's incredible qualities inspire and guide you from a place of simply surviving to thriving.

Through relatable stories and powerful insights learn to embrace unconditional love, foster deeper connections, stay committed to your dreams and cherish every precious moment. Practical exercises are included in each chapter to empower you to embody and express the remarkable qualities of dogs in your daily life, leading to real and lasting transformation.

Embrace the journey. Embrace yourself. Embrace life.

Printed in Great Britain
by Amazon

33488037R00086